NORTHWEST LEGACY

SAIL, STEAM & MOTORSHIPS

A Century of Maritime Photographs

JEREMY S. SNAPP

FOREWORD BY GERALD S. SNAPP

PACIFIC NORTHWEST HERITAGE PRESS

Published by
PACIFIC NORTHWEST HERITAGE PRESS
479 Old Homestead Road
Lopez Island, WA 98261

Drawing on page 7 by Gerald Snapp

Design by Jeremy Snapp

Edited by Marge Mueller

Production and typesetting by Gray Mouse Graphics

Printed in Singapore on acid-free paper

ISBN 0-9673633-1-4

CONTENTS

FOREWORD

AFTER THE END OF WORLD WAR II, the ship on which I was serving was directed to North Island shipyard in San Francisco Bay for decommissioning and for discharge of the ship's company. One of the crew was asked where he intended to live after eighteen months at sea. He replied, "I'm headed inland with an anchor and I'll settle down in the first place where someone asks me what it is for."

All of us looked forward to putting our sea legs on dry land. We had no regrets at leaving behind cramped quarters, watch standing, Navy discipline, ordinary meals, continual drills, paint chipping, and other assorted delights.

Or so we thought!

At a recent reunion of the remnants of the ship's company—landlubbers who were thrown together in the great adventure of navigating the Pacific—we couldn't stop the flow of stories of distant voyages that both threatened and beguiled us. All hands present would readily admit it was the greatest event in their lives.

Ships and the sea have the ability to affect some deep-down emotions that cannot be explained. It is like trying to describe the smell of salt air, or the deep hum of a gale force storm in the rigging, or the mournful sound of a foghorn, or the "chuckling" noise that water makes against the hull of a ship as she moves slowly to a slip.

For those of you who love the sea and its many faces, this book will more than just whet your appetite. The first few photographs reveal an age of seafaring that existed at the beginning of the twentieth century. But by the time the last page is turned, these photos will have imprinted your mind with ghosts of stalwart, hard-working ships past, and images of those present.

Jeremy Snapp returns us to a time when roads were almost nonexistent, and waterways were our highways. The "Mosquito Fleet" linked the docks of various communities, towns, and cities to each other and to the world. Farmers rowed across Admiralty Inlet to sell their eggs and produce, freight trains were barged to a distant railhead, naval vessels were dry-docked in Bremerton, and Alaska's inside passage became a commercial bonanza. The steamer *Flyer* made daily trips between downtown Tacoma and Seattle in an hour (about the same time it now takes to drive the distance on a good day). In Seattle, a ship canal gouged from the earth linked fresh water to saltwater.

The inland waters served up a banquet filled with fishing fleets, log rafts, woodchip barges, pile drivers, tugs, yachts, ferries, freighters, ocean liners, and battleships. Whirling about the edges, like little children, were the small craft—Indian canoes, skiffs, dories, wherries, Navy "liberty" barges, and pleasure sailboats.

Such is this reunion of memories of ships that became a significant part of the growth of our Pacific Northwest. On these pages visit them in their anchorages, vicariously walk their decks . . . smell the salt air.

The Reverend Gerald S. Snapp
Lt. Comdr. USNR (Ret.)

INTRODUCTION

W HEN I WAS YOUR AGE," my grandfather would tell me, "I worked on the largest steamship ever built, the SS *Minnesota*. I spent my fourteenth birthday in Hong Kong." This and other sea stories were repeated to me during the summers I worked for Grandpa John at the family's summer home near Hansville, Washington. Grandpa John was a bit of a curmudgeon, and had little patience for his grandkids in his later years, expecting us to live up to his childhood drive and Victorian-era standards. He did double my salary from fifty cents to a dollar an hour during my second summer, so he must have thought I had a little potential. With his guidance over the years I learned my way around various machines, boats, tractors, and many hand tools. At ages fourteen and fifteen I built a couple of boats in his shop.

My grandfather, John Farrington Snapp, was born in 1897 in St. Paul, Minnesota, where his grandfather, Col. Farrington, was a celebrated fur trapper. In 1901 his father, John Linton Snapp, moved the family to Seattle, where he had a job as a right-of-way agent for James Hill's Great Northern Railway. At the age of thirteen my grandfather shipped out on the Great Northern Steamship Company's SS *Minnesota* on its run to the Orient. He signed on as a telephone boy; the job consisted of operating the ship's telephone exchange. This voyage lasted two months and sixteen days and he was paid a total salary of $25.33, $19.50 of which was taken out to pay for uniforms, leaving a net pay of $5.83.

The SS *Minnesota* and its sistership the *Dakota* (which foundered in 1906) were built in Connecticut by Eastern Shipbuilding Co. Each were of 20,718 tons–the largest ships built in the U.S. at the time. About 40,000 people attended the *Minnesota's* launching in 1903, and she arrived at Seattle via Cape Horn in December of 1904. On her second voyage to the Orient, besides thousands of tons of general cargo, she carried seventy steam locomotives, and could accommodate about 1800 passengers. However, she consumed tremendous amounts of coal in the process: 200 to 300 tons a day.

From the time he was a teenager, until World War II, my grandfather owned a succession of power boats, the *Betty*, *Betty II*, and *Betty III*, in which he cruised extensively and photographed Puget Sound. During World War I he joined the Navy and was a machinist mate on a 110-foot subchaser along the Pacific coast; he saw limited action in 1918 near Mazatalan, Mexico. In 1921 he married Elizabeth Hallock Sherman and in 1929 they bought a farm at Hansville, where they spent their summers. After the war he continued working around ships, this time as a broker of marine insurance. His business grew to eventually require the help of his three sons.

The Great Northern Steamship Company's SS *Minnesota*, of 1903

John Snapp in Yokohama, 1911.

All his life he was an avid photographer; he carried a camera wherever he went during the war, on business and on boats. Starting with a Kodak Autographic, he later used different Zeiss, Rollieflex and Leica cameras. His love of photography was passed down to family members; I remember receiving my first camera at the age of six. We all kept photo albums, which at the slightest excuse we would show to family and friends. The result of this interest has been the accumulation of tens of thousands of photos by my grandfather (1910 to 1970) and myself (1960 to 1999). Though it was a long process to look over these negatives to decide which ones to use here, some stood out at first glance.

This book does not attempt to tell the complete story of the past century of Northwest maritime history. Rather, my grandfather and I simply captured scenes from our daily lives alongshore and on the waters of the Pacific Northwest. I don't care to use the term "take" a picture, and feel that some of our best photographs were not taken, but given to us. Many times we simply recorded what came our way.

Jeremy Snapp, 1999

DEDICATION

TO GERALD SHERMAN SNAPP,

WHO UNSELFISHLY GAVE SO MUCH
TO SO MANY PEOPLE THROUGHOUT HIS LIFE.

– IN MEMORIAM –
1923–1999

ACKNOWLEDGMENTS

I WOULD LIKE TO THANK the many people who gave so generously of their time. Without their help, information would not have been available on many photographs. I'd also like to thank my wife and three children who put up with me during this project; my Mother and Father who gave me my first camera when I was six, supplied me with film, and kept my grandfather's negative collection together; and Grandpa John who produced so many wonderful images over a period of more than sixty years.

The following people gave help generously: Marge Mueller, who did her best to keep me on course; Capt. Keith Sternberg, my neighbor, marine machinist, and compass adjuster who is so knowledgeable about the ways of the Northwest waterfront; Capt. Harold Huycke, author and marine historian; James G. McCurdy, past president of Puget Sound Bridge and Drydock Co.; Gary White, expert on Hall Brothers ships; Capt. Ed Shields, the last skipper of a west coast cod fishing schooner and marine historian; Tom Lovejoy, grandson of Capt. Frank Lovejoy and now at the helm of Puget Sound Freight Lines, now Puget Sound Truck Lines; Lieter Hocket, retired salvage diver and marine historian; Anchor Jensen and his son DeWitt Jensen of Jensen Motorboat Company; R.B. "Buck" Plummer who worked on the steam tug *Tyee* and other vessels; Capt. Dave Webb, Coast Guard historian; C.W. "Bill" Somers, who worked on so many Mosquito Fleet steamers and has the delightful Museum of Puget Sound near Grapeview; Capt. Steve Mayo, a marine historian and noted watercolor artist; Frank Clapp, marine historian in Victoria, B.C.; Mark Freeman and his son Erik Freeman, tugboat historians; and my son Trevor Snapp who helped so much with the photo research. I offer many thanks. I also take full responsibility for any errors and omissions, and welcome correspondence from anyone on this subject, sent to the address shown on the copyright page.

SAILING SHIPS SUCH AS THIS GERMAN FOUR-MASTED BARK *THIELBEK,* of 2831 tons, were a dying breed when this photo was made. The *Thielbek* was built in 1893 as the *Prince Robert* by T. Royden and Sons of Liverpool, England. Here she is on August 22, 1913, waiting on the Columbia River for a tow to the wharf, most likely to take on a load of grain. Like many square riggers built in the 1890s, she is rigged with double topgallants, has a large deckhouse amidships and a turtleback aft to prevent the helmsman from being washed overboard by a following sea when running before the wind. Two days after this photo was made, the *Thielbek,* in tow of the Columbia River steamer *Ocklahama,* collided with the Norwegian steamer *Thode Fagelund.* A year later the *Thielbek* was with a group of vessels caught in Mexico at the outbreak of World War I. The ship remained there until after the war, when she was purchased by Robert Dollar & Co., brought up to San Francisco, and renamed the *David Dollar.* She ended her days as part of a breakwater near Oakland.

THE NORWEGIAN THREE-MASTED BARK, *MARCO POLO,* is shown on the Columbia River, July 19, 1913. This vessel of 1620 tons was built by Grangemouth Dockyard Co. in Great Britain in 1892, and is shown here in tow of the stern paddlewheel steamer *Ocklahama.* The *Ocklahama,* 676 tons, was the first sternwheeler on the Columbia River used solely for towing. During her active career, from 1875 to 1930, she towed more ships than any other vessel. Like many steamers with a long life she suffered her share of accidents, including being crushed by the unballasted bark *Alliance* capsizing on top of her in 1886. Completely rebuilt from 1894 to 1897, she was with the Port of Portland until 1916, then was owned by Western Transportation Co. until 1930.

THE DOWNEASTER SHIP *ELWELL* (right), of 1461 tons, was built in Damariscotta, Maine, in 1875, and was home ported in San Francisco for many years. She was purchased by the George T. Meyers Canning Co. in 1909, her rig was reduced, and she was converted to a fish processor.

THE *ELWELL* LIES READY for the 1916 Alaskan fishing season (overleaf). Although she has sails bent, a new towing hawser is coiled on her fo'c'sle head. Note the chain-driven anchor windlass. Behind her are buildings of the Pacific Mildcure Co. and most likely their two-masted schooner *Volante,* of 1891, in the background. About a year after this photo was made the *Volante* was lost during a storm in Chatham Straits, Alaska. The *Elwell* burned in 1932.

WITH THE STEAM TENDER *PHILLIP C. KELLY* LYING ALONGSIDE, and steam pressure up to turn the capstan, the crew of the *Elwell* employs their ship's gear lifting from the main yard to hoist the *Kelly's* spare propeller and stow it in the hold.

THE AUXILIARY SCHOONER *RUBY*, of 345 tons (right), was purchased by Capt. J. E. Shields and Capt. Louis Knaflich, and brought north from Bandon, Oregon, in 1914. In May of that year she was chartered by the Hudson Bay Co. to take supplies and tow a 65-foot launch to Herschel Island in the Arctic Ocean, and from there up the Mackenzie River. For many years she was used by the Kuskokwim Fishing and Transportation Co. to transport cargo between Seattle and Alaska's Kuskokwim River. She retired to Lake Union in Seattle, and after a number of years was sold to Spike Africa and his partners for possible charter work. In May of 1938, the *Ruby* was bought by the Suryan Packing Co. of Anacortes, Washington, after their barge sank at the American Can Co. dock. The vessel was derigged and converted to a barge, and just one week after her purchase departed for Alaska loaded with 400 tons of cans and other cargo for the company's cannery near Juneau.

THE FIVE-MASTED BARKENTINE, *FOREST PRIDE*, 1,600 tons, is shown here under tow of two tugs, returning from a salvage operation in southeast Alaska. She was built in Aberdeen, Washington, in 1919 as part of the World War I fleet buildup. However, she was finished too late to serve during the war. In 1934 she was purchased by Curtis Bros., a house moving company, to help in the salvage of the long-sunken wreck of the steamship *Islander*. The steamship, operated by Canadian Pacific Railway, had gone down near Taku Inlet on August 15, 1901 with a loss of forty-two lives. Although it was long believed that the *Islander* contained a lot of gold, none was found, and the operation was not considered a financial success. Even the whiskey bottles suffered from saltwater intrusion; however, several cases of champagne were found to be fresh and bubbly.

MANY WOODEN VESSELS LAID UP IN LAKE UNION every winter for two reasons: Freshwater would kill wood-boring worms that damaged the hulls, and moorage was free. Shown in the photo at right, from left to right, are the *Sophie Christenson, Charles R. Wilson, C. A. Thayer, Forest Pride, K.V. Kruse,* and *La Merced.*

The 675 ton, four-masted schooner *Sophie Christensen* was built in 1901 by Hall Bros. Shipyard at Port Blakely, Washington, for the lumber trade. One of the swiftest schooners of her time, the *Christensen* established a record of fifty-seven days from Puget Sound to Callao, Peru. Capt. J.E. Shields, purchased the schooner for use in the lumber trade in 1925, but in 1929 she was converted to work as a Bering Sea codfisher. She was later bought by Gibson Bros. Logging Co. of British Columbia, to be used as a barge to haul logs out of Tahsis on Vancouver Island, and was wrecked there in the mid-fifties.

The *Charles R. Wilson,* of 345 tons, was built by Danish-born Hans D. Bendixsen at Fairhaven, California, in 1891, and was bought by the newly-organized Pacific Codfish Co. in 1912. She fished for cod until 1947, and was the only schooner to fish during World War II. In 1954 she was beached at Stillwater, British Columbia.

The 453-ton *C. A. Thayer*, launched in 1895, was another Bendixsen-built lumber schooner. After suffering serious damage in a storm, she was bought by Pete Nelson in 1912 for use as a supply ship for his salmon salteries in Alaska. In 1925 the schooner was purchased by Capt. J.E. Shields of the Pacific Codfish Co., and was used for five years in the Bering Sea cod fishery. During the Depression the *Thayer* was laid up in Seattle's Lake Union, but with the advent of World War II she

was requisitioned by the U.S. Army, her masts removed, and she was put to work in British Columbia as an ammunition barge. Following the war, the vessel was repurchased by Shields, refitted with masts, and returned to codfishing. Her final season was 1950, in command of Capt. Ed Shields, giving her the distinction of being the last cod fishing schooner to fish the Bering Sea. After being beached for a number of years at Lilliwaup, on Washington's Hood Canal, in 1957 Capt. Harold Huycke negotiated the sale of the *Thayer* to the State of California for use as a museum ship. After preliminary restoration in Winslow, she was sailed to San Francisco in command of Capt. Adrian F. Raynaud and a crew of volunteers. The restored schooner is now on display at the San Francisco Maritime National Historical Park (see page 188).

The *K. V. Kruse,* a five-masted schooner of 1,728 tons, was built in 1920 by Kruse and Banks Shipyard in North Bend, Oregon. After carrying cargo through the 1920s, including voyages to Australia, she was laid up at Astoria, Oregon, from 1930 until being sold to Seattle shipbreakers Nieder and Marcus in 1935. However, the vessel was found to be in good condition, and she was later sold to Gibson Bros. Logging Co. for use as a log barge in British Columbia; her days ended in 1940 when she was lost in the Hecate Straits in British Columbia.

The four-masted auxiliary schooner *La Merced,* of 1,696 tons, was built for World War I service and saw duty in France. Later owned by the Columbia River Smoked Fish Co., she was converted to a salmon saltery by Alaska Southern Packing Co. in 1927, and then used as a floating cannery at Port Moller, Alaska, by the Peninsula Packing Co. Retiring as a cannery ship about 1950, she lay in Seattle's Lake Union for a number of years before being towed to Anacortes, Washington, and becoming a part of Tony Lovric's breakwater.

THE FOUR-MASTED SCHOONER *C.S. HOLMES* is seen here at an Elliott Bay pier in Seattle with booms raised to prepare for loading cargo. At 409 tons, she was one of the smallest four-masted schooners. Note the large deckhouse, which was added for increased cargo capacity. Built in 1893 by the Hall Bros. at Port Blakely on Bainbridge Island, she was hull number 77, of 115 total. She was named after an owner of the Port Blakely Mill Co. The *Holmes* was probably the last schooner to sail commercially out of Puget Sound. Her career ended when she was requisitioned by the Army in 1942, demasted and reduced to a barge. Severely hogged at the war's end, she finished her days in British Columbia.

WINTERING IN SEATTLE, THE *C.S. HOLMES* lies at the Foss Launch and Tug Co. moorings January 22, 1938. Capt. John Backland Sr. purchased the *Holmes* after loosing his schooner *Transit* in the ice in 1913. Born in Sweden in 1870, Capt. Backland was an Alaskan Arctic trader. When he became ill in 1928 his son, Capt. John Backland Jr., took over the operation of his business, the Midnight Sun Trading Co. Note the wonderful acanthus leaf scrollwork carved into her fiddlehead, or billethead. This scrollwork was traditionally gilded or painted yellow or white. In 1922 Capt. Roald Amundsen used the *C.S. Holmes* as an auxiliary ship for his famous Arctic expedition.

THE SCHOONER *COMMODORE*, of 1526 tons, seen here October 1941, was built in 1919 by J.H. Price at Seattle. This vessel and the 1,603-ton schooner *Vigilant,* built at Hoquiam in 1920, were the last sailing ships to carry lumber out of Puget Sound. The *Commodore* retired from this trade in 1935. However, in 1941 she was rerigged, loaded with lumber at Port Angeles and on December 20, 1941 sailed for Durban, South Africa, where she arrived the following May. After her arrival and discharge of lumber, she was completely disassembled and the salvaged wood was used in the construction of new homes.

THESE CHARLES NELSON AND CO. SHIPS, which all took part in the late 1920s shipping boom, await an uncertain future. Like many other vessels involved in commercial sail, at this time, during the Depression, the six-masted schooner *Fort Laramie,* 2240 gt, the five-masted barkentine *Monitor,* 2247 gt, and the five-masted schooner *Thistle,* 1586 gt, were not able to find cargoes. The two World War I schooners were burned for their metal at Richmond Beach on Puget Sound in 1935; the barkentine was converted into a fish reduction plant and later scrapped.

THE *ALUMNA*, A FOUR-MASTED SCHOONER of 696 tons, was built in 1901 by K.V. Kruse at Marshfield, in North Bend, Oregon, for the Simpson Lumber Co. In 1933 she was purchased by McGinitie and McDonald and, minus one mast, was converted to a floating brewery for the Pilsner Brewing Co. of Ketchikan, Alaska. She arrived there in late 1934 in tow of the steamer *Akutan*. She was later converted to a fish processor.

THE B.B. CROWNINSHIELD-DESIGNED AUXILIARY SCHOONER *ADVENTURESS*, 78 tons, prepares for a landing at Port Townsend, Washington, in September of 1979. Topmasts were stepped a few years later, which finished her rig rebuilding. She was launched at the Rice Brothers yard, East Boothbay, Maine, in 1913 and sailed around Cape Horn to the Pacific Northwest that same year. She was used by John Borden II for whaling and big game expeditions in Arctic waters. In 1915 Borden sold her to the San Francisco bar pilots, and she served them until 1951, along with the schooner *Gracie S.* Borden then had a larger 140-foot three-masted schooner, the *Great Bear*, built for Arctic use; however she foundered near St. Matthew Island on her maiden voyage, August 10, 1916.

After many years of use as a San Francisco pilot schooner the *Adventuress* was replaced by a Navy surplus minesweeper; she then languished on the beach for many years at Sausilito. O.H. "Doc" Freeman sailed her up the coast to Seattle about 1960, and soon thereafter she was sold to Youth Adventures for use as a sail training schooner, as seen here. An enthusiastic Ernestine Bennett, "Mrs. B," became head of Youth Adventures in 1974, overseeing the restoration of the *Adventuress* over the years. The schooner was designated a National Historic Landmark on April 11, 1989. In 1991 she was sold to Sound Experience for use in environmental education and sail training, and as of 1999 is based in Port Townsend.

THE AUXILIARY SCHOONER *ZODIAC*, WILLIAM HAND DESIGNED, was built at East Boothbay, Maine in 1924. She arrived at San Francisco in 1932, was purchased by the San Francisco Pilots, and was rigged and renamed *California*. She was used as a pilot schooner for the next forty years. Retired about 1972, she wound up in Newport, Oregon and was purchased by the Mehrer family about 1975. Capt. Carl Mehrer (who earlier had helped restore the *Adventuress*) brought the *Zodiac* north to Seattle and led the effort to restore her, with help from his family and many volunteers. The rerigged schooner first sailed in 1988, and since 1991 has been used for sail training charters.

THE AUXILIARY SCHOONER *ALCYONE,* right, was designed by noted shipwright Frank Prothero, who built the vessel in his backyard. Launched in 1956, 29 tons, she was used by Prothero for about nine years, and then was sold to Peter and Sue Hanke. John "Sugar" Flanagan purchased the schooner in 1987 and with his wife Leslie have lived aboard since, cruising extensively, including a two-year voyage through the South Pacific from 1994-96. The *Alcyone* is presently being used for sail training charters.

TWO REPLICAS, THE BARK *ENDEAVOUR* AND THE BRIG *LADY WASHINGTON* (right), visited Northwest ports in 1999, giving many people the unique opportunity to experience an eighteenth-century ship. Both the original vessels explored the Pacific Northwest about the same time, American Capt. Robert Gray arriving with the *Lady Washington* in 1788, and English Capt. James Cook arriving in the *Endeavour* about a decade earlier. Construction of both the replicas commenced about the same time, in the late 1980s. The *Endeavour* replica, 397 tons, was built at Fremantle, Australia, with the support of the Australian National Maritime Museum, private corporations, and the National Maritime Museum, Greenwich. The *Lady Washington* replica, 99 tons, was built in Washington state at Grays Harbor Historical Seaport, at the confluence of the Chehalis and Wishkah Rivers, with the support of corporations, local governments, and hometown folks. Though not the genuine article, both are as close as one will get today. They represent incredible effort and teach something about history and goodwill.

THE SAIL-TRAINING SCHOONERS *ROBERTSON II* AND *PACIFIC SWIFT* (overleaf) lie at the Sail and Life Training Society (SALTS) shipyard at Victoria, B.C. for the winter season. The *Robertson II*, was built in Nova Scotia in 1940, and fished the Grand Banks for a number of years before being brought out to Victoria, British Columbia, in 1974.

A REPLICA OF THE *ROBERTSON II,* THE *PACIFIC GRACE,* is under construction at the SALTS shipyard. In this deck view, the fo'c'sle scuttle has been framed in and the forward companionway framework has been started. Note the notches in the port and starboard deckbeams to accept an extra thick deck plank, which helps lock in the deck and prevent any movement.

THE CURVED ELLIPTICAL TRANSOM TAKES SHAPE, and the planking is nearly finished. This vessel is being constructed to the highest standards with the best quality Douglas-fir. Launching is planned for October 1999, and with a little care the *Pacific Grace* could live until the twenty-second century.

THE THREE-MASTED BARKENTINE *REGINA MARIS* was built as the 144-foot three-masted schooner *Regina* by Jorgen Ring-Andersen at Svendborg, Denmark in 1908. She was busy transporting cargoes throughout the Baltic for 37 years, and in 1945 was converted to a Grand Banks codfishing schooner based in Sweden. In 1960 she was laid up, then was converted to a barkentine in 1963 by the Wilson brothers of Norway, who dreamed of sailing a square-rigged ship around Cape Horn. Three years later she became the first wooden cargo sailing ship in about sixty years to round the horn. From 1976 until 1987 she was owned by the Ocean Research Education Society which used her to study whales, and then fell on hard times. She now is moored at Glen Cove, N.Y., awaiting another restoration.

THE *WANDER BIRD*, A FORMER PILOT SCHOONER, was built by Gustav Junge at Wevelsfleth, Germany in 1883 as *Elbe 5*, and for forty-one years carried pilots to ships entering the Elbe River to travel to Hamburg or Cuxhaven. She was retired in 1924 and was later renamed *Wandervogel*. Warwick Tompkins purchased her in 1928 and renamed her *Wander Bird*. She was restored, then sailed for many years. The Tompkins' eventually brought her to San Francisco in 1936 by way of Cape Horn. After deteriorating over time, she was restored by Harold Sommer and friends in the 1970's, and in 1981 sailed for the first time in forty years. Purchased by Seattle partners, she sailed up the coast, arriving in the Northwest in the fall of 1998. The schooner is seen here on Seattle's Lake Union.

A FORMER UNIVERSITY OF WASHINGTON RESEARCH VESSEL, THE *CATALYST*, gets some annual maintenance at Port Townsend, Washington. Built in Seattle in 1932, of 91 tons, and fitted out as a laboratory for the University of Washington, she assisted in oceanographic research for ten years, until she was requisitioned by the U.S. Navy for use during World War II. In 1950 the *Catalyst* was sold to J. H. Scott and Co. of San Francisco for transporting ore from Hyder, in southeast Alaska, to the Asarco Smelter in Tacoma. Today, she still runs with her original six-cylinder, 120-hp Washington diesel, and takes passengers to southeast Alaska to do their own research. Years ago her deckhouses were modified a bit, and she now measures out at 102 tons.

ANOTHER ALASKA VETERAN, THE *WESTWARD*, was designed by L.E. (Ted) Geary on lines similar to a cannery tender. Of 96 tons, she was built at Dockton on Vashon Island, Washington, in 1924 for the Alaska Coast Hunting and Cruising Co. The *Westward* and the *Catalyst*, on the opposite page, are both now managed by Tom George and Kit Africa of the Pacific Catalyst Co. The *Westward* is still powered by her original Atlas diesel.

THE *WESTWARD'S* 110-HP ATLAS IMPERIAL DIESEL, receives some needed maintenance after nearly seventy-five years of use, which included a world circumnavigation. Her engineer, Bob Dubois, prepares to reinstall her number-four piston in the twelve-foot-long, eight-ton engine. With proper care these heavy-duty diesels can run about 100, 000 hours before needing major work.

Pacific Northwest Tugboats HAVE PLAYED AN IMPORTANT PART

in Northwest History ever since 1837, when the steam sidewheeler *Beaver* arrived here. The Foss Launch and Tug Co. Seattle moorings, shown above, shared much of that history. Andrew Foss and Thea Christanson met at the Norwegian port of Christiana. Foss had been born as Andrew Olesen in 1855 at Skirfoss, and his wife-to-be was born in 1858 at Eidesberg. In 1881 they both immigrated to St. Paul, Minnesota, where they married. Andrew changed his name to Foss, as there were so many Olesens in St. Paul. In 1888 the couple settled in Tacoma, Washington. One day, while Andrew was off building a house, his wife purchased a rowboat for five dollars from a disgruntled fisherman. She was able to resell this boat for fifteen dollars and reinvest the money in two more rowboats, which, instead of being resold, were rented out.

The Fosses parlayed this humble beginning into the Foss Launch and Tug Co., based in Tacoma. In 1920 they purchased the Rouse Tugboat Co. and started a Seattle division at the Rouse site in Ballard. In 1930 the entire operation was moved to the company's present location on the southwest side of Salmon Bay in Seattle. The company is now known as Foss Maritime. The four-masted schooner is the *C.S. Holmes*.

THE STEAM TUG *WALLOWA*, built in 1889 for the Oregon Railroad and Navigation Co. 214 tons, was designed by David Stephenson of Portland to work as a bar tug on the mouth of the Columbia River. She was fitted with a Union Iron Works (San Francisco) two-cylinder compound steam engine of 122 hp. During the 1898 Klondike Gold Rush she towed steamers and barges from Seattle to Skagway for the Pacific Clipper Line. She was later purchased by Merrill and Ring Lumber Co. of Port Angeles for towing log booms, then was acquired by the Foss Launch and Tug Co. in 1929.

The *Wallowa's* most unusual career turn came when she became a movie star, appearing in the 1933 film "Tugboat Annie," playing the role of the *Narcissus* with actress Marie Dressler as her captain. In 1934 a 700-hp Washington diesel was installed and she was renamed the *Arthur Foss*. This enormous 6-cylinder, 65-ton diesel, has a bore of 18 inches and a stroke of 24 inches. In 1964 the tug was again renamed, this time *Theodore Foss*, as a giant new 5000-hp tug was to be christened *Arthur Foss*. She was retired by Foss in 1968, and in 1970 the company donated her to Northwest Seaport, which now maintains the historic vessel in excellent working condition and displays it at harbors around the Pacific Northwest. Her 1934 Washington diesel is still running strong today.

THE *DREW FOSS*, shown here towing several sections of flat boom, is typical of the smaller tugs that worked on inland waters of the Northwest. Of 34 tons, she was built in 1929 by the Foss Launch and Tug Co. at their Tacoma shipyard. She is still going today, and is moored at Victoria, British Columbia.

THE *LORNA FOSS* MOTORS TOWARD THE BALLARD BRIDGE, past logs boomed near the Seattle Shingle Mill. Built at Hoquiam as the steam tug *Pilot*, in 1903 for Polson Lumber Co., she was purchased by Foss Launch and Tug Co. about 1924. She was repowered with a 150-hp Eastern Standard diesel, and used by Foss from 1924 to 1958. In 1971 marine engineer Dan Grinstead of Ace Tugboat Co. acquired her. She is presently powered by a six-cylinder, 120 hp direct reversing Atlas Imperial diesel.

THIS LITTLE MILL TUG has just enough snoose to nudge this section of large fir logs down the Squak Slough, connecting Lake Sammamish to Lake Washington, in 1915.

THE TUG *FISH* IS UP ON THE WAYS for a little caulking. This 40-foot vessel of 11 tons was built at Empire City, Oregon, in 1903. When this photograph was made on April 21, 1935, she had a 60-hp diesel and was owned by the General Construction Co. She is under restoration in Seattle today.

THE LARGE STEEL OCEAN STEAM TUG *HUMACONNA* (right) is seen here at Lake Union Drydock. She was built in 1919, of 418 tons, and had a 1000-hp steam engine. After three years of use by the shipping board she was purchased by the Cary-Davis Towing Co. in 1921, and was later used by the Merrill and Ring Lumber Co. of Port Angeles for towing log booms. In the 1950s she was purchased by the Western Pacific Railway Co. for moving railroad car barges in San Francisco Bay.

THE STEAMSHIP *ROOSEVELT,* (overleaf) had a varied and illustrious career. She was built in 1905 at Vernon, Maine, as an Arctic exploration ship and rigged as a three-masted auxiliary schooner. The *Roosevelt* served as Admiral Robert Peary's flagship on his famous expedition, which succeeded in reaching the North Pole in 1909. The steamer was purchased by Washington Tug and Barge Co. and was modified for deep sea towing, but kept some of the original sailing rig. At the time she was considered one of the most powerful steam tugs in the Northwest. In 1933, a year before this photo was made, the *Roosevelt* towed 21 million board feet of logs to San Diego in three huge, 1,000-foot-long Bensen rafts. She is shown at Seattle's Pier 40, later Pier 90. This is where the *President Madison* broke loose during the Octover 1934 storm, and caused extensive damage (see page 120).

THE STEAM TUG *WANDERER*, 212 tons, is seen here at Lake Union Dry Dock in Seattle, in 1933. Designed by Winslow Hall and launched in 1890, she was the only tug the Hall brothers built at Port Blakely. Her steam engine was built by Willamette Iron and Steel and shipped up to the Hall Bros. Shipyard from Oregon, and her Scotch boiler was built in Seattle. The Hall Bros. built wooden ships in three different Puget Sound locations, from 1873 to 1880 in Port Ludlow, 1881 to 1903 in Port Blakely, and 1904 to 1915 in Eagle Harbor at Winslow.

THE *WANDERER* WAS PART OF A TUGBOAT POOL formed in 1891 by four of the largest sawmills on Puget Sound. This group eventually became the Puget Sound Tugboat Co. The Puget Mill Co. contributed the *Tyee*, built in Port Ludlow for Pope and Talbot in 1884; the Washington Mill Co., the *Richard Holyoke*, built at Seabeck in 1887; the Tacoma Mill Co., the *Tacoma*; and the Port Blakely Mill Co., the *Wanderer*, built at Port Blakely in 1890. At the time, these four steamers were considered very modern vessels, boasting screw propellers instead of paddlewheels and burning coal instead of wood. Note the chainfall rigged from her stern to assist in rudder repair.

THE TUG *TYEE* WAS BUILT AT HOQUIAM, WASHINGTON, in 1925 for the Allman-Hubble Tug Boat Co. The 90-ton tug originally had a 340-hp steam engine, but in 1930 she was repowered with a 500-hp diesel. Three years later she was stranded at Brighton, Oregon, and after a tremendous effort by Ballard Marine Railway, which moved the vessel a thousand feet across the beach, she was refloated. In 1940 she was blown ashore on the Tillamook Bar in Oregon, and was later bought and refloated by Foss Launch and Tug Co., and renamed the *Sandra Foss*.

THE *WANDERER* (left) was bought by Merrill and Ring Lumber Co. of Port Angeles, Washington, in 1916. She was acquired by the Foss Co. in 1936 and at 128 feet was the largest tug in their fleet. Foss installed a new boiler, increased the steam pressure a bit and was able to obtain 800 hp from the old Willamette engine, up from its original 511 hp. The *Wanderer* moved the massive concrete pontoons for the first Lake Washington floating bridge—a structure that in time put many steamships out of business. Retired by Foss in 1947, she was abandoned on the Nisqually mud flats south of Tacoma in 1950.

THE TUG *MELVILLE* STARTED LIFE AS A PASSENGER STEAMER for the Callender Navigation Co. The 79-ton vessel, equipped with a 220 hp steam engine, was built in 1903 at Knappton, Washington. Taken over by the Knappton Towboat Co. of Astoria, her engine was removed in 1930 and replaced by a 440-hp diesel. She is seen here in March of 1936 passing the docks of the Puget Sound Bridge and Dredging Co. While based in Portland in 1948, the *Melville* made a heroic rescue of a 500-foot escort carrier which, after being torn from her moorings by a loose log raft, careened down the Willamette River.

THE PUGET SOUND TUG AND BARGE STEAM TUG *SNOHOMISH*, a former U.S. revenue cutter, was built by Pusey and Jones at Wilmington, Delaware in 1908. She arrived on station that same year and operated out of Port Angeles and Neah Bay on the Strait of Juan de Fuca. The 795-ton vessel with a triple expansion steam engine of 1,400 hp, made fourteen knots, and was equipped with the latest lifesaving and rescue gear, including a seven-inch suction pump and a Lyle gun. After a twenty-six year career saving lives and ships, she was sold to Puget Sound Tug and Barge Co. Just after this photo was made, in 1937, she was sold to Island Tug and Barge Co. of Victoria, British Columbia, and soon thereafter towed the old Alaska Packers' *Star of Holland* up from San Francisco for use as a log barge.

THE PUGET SOUND BRIDGE AND DREDGING CO.'S *MACRAY,* an 86-ton former cannery tender, tows a company barge. She was named after H.W. "Mac" McCurdy and Ray Huff, the president and vice-president of PSB&D.

THE STEAM TUG *MASTER* is the last survivor of three wooden sister tugs of 93 tons built at Beach Avenue Shipyard, Vancouver, British Columbia, by master builder Arthur Moscrop in 1922. The *Master's* triple-expansion steam engine was purchased surplus from the Royal Navy after World War I. With the engine producing approximately 350 indicated hp and turning an 8-foot-diameter propeller 100 rpm, at 175 psi, the *Master* makes a good eight knots. The Steam Tug *Master* Society keeps her in excellent working order, getting steam up throughout the year. She is usually based at the Vancouver B.C. Maritime Museum.

NEEDING IMMEDIATE ATTENTION, THE *MADRONA* languishes near Anacortes, Washington in the late 1990s. The 28-ton tug was built at Tacoma in 1923 for Olson Tug Boat Co. In 1965 this vessel, along with the *Paddy Craig,* was acquired from Olson by Halvorsen Towing Co. of Winslow.

THE 31-TON TUG *CREOSOTE* lies at the Fishing Vessel Owners dock at Seattle's Fishermans Terminal. She was built in Seattle in 1921 for the Pacific Creosoting Co. of Eagle Harbor, Bainbridge Island and later was owned by the Wyckoff Co. In 1963 she was rebuilt and repowered at the Duwamish Shipyard. In the background is the boat shop of shipwrights Joe Bakketun and John Thomas, who are working on the motor yacht *Malibu*, whose wheelhouse is just visible in the photo.

THE 92-TON *SAMSON* steams up the Baranof Island shore toward Samson Tug and Barge Co. at Sitka, Alaska. This former U.S. Navy tug was rebuilt for service in southeast Alaska in 1961, and has been based there ever since.

THE TUG *JERRIE*, 71 tons, also of the Samson Tug and Barge Co., steams north out of Sitka, Alaska. She is a former cannery tender.

THE TUG *KIKET*, has a long history in the Pacific Northwest. She was built at Astoria, Oregon, in 1890, and began her working career as the 117-ton cannery steamer *R.P. Elmore* for the S. Elmore Canning Co. Eight years later she was acquired by the American Tug Boat Co., of Everett, the first of many tugs they were to own. In 1922 she was completely rebuilt, renumbered, remeasured, and renamed the *Elmore*. She then measured 87 tons, and employed the first Washington-Estep diesel from Washington Iron Works of Seattle. Washington Estep diesels were manufactured from 1922 to 1931, when the company slightly redesigned their line of heavy duty diesels. They built a total of some 350 diesel engines. She was renamed the *Kiket*, and about 1968 was acquired by Puget Sound Freight Lines, and was used for towing the 156-foot barges *Skagit* and *Dungeness*, with 1,200 tons of newsprint, between Canada's Powell River and Seattle. Eventually sold by Puget Sound Freight Lines, this tug is presently based at Eagledale, Washington, and has been renamed the *Elmore* (see page 210). The *Elmore* and the *Arthur Foss* are the only vessels surviving today that participated in the Klondike Gold Rush.

THE *DOLLY C*, SHOWN HERE TOWING THE *DAVID W. BRANCH* through Seattle's Ballard locks into her Lake Union moorage, was built in 1922 at Dockton on Vashon Island, Washington. She had been commissioned for the Olympic Tug and Barge Co., but before the vessel was launched, she was taken over by Cary-Davis Towing Co. She was later owned by Puget Sound Tug and Barge Co. and used by them until 1954, when she foundered in the Straits of Juan de Fuca near Whidbey Island.

PACIFIC NORTHWEST STEAMERS WERE AN IMPORTANT TRANSPORTATION LINK in 1912, as evidenced by these steamer docks at Victoria Harbor (overleaf). Viewed from about the third story of the Empress Hotel, the Canadian Pacific Railway docks are at far left, factories and dock are at Laurel Point (center), and the Evans, Coleman and Evans, and Grand Trunk Pacific docks are at right. Note the horse-drawn wagons driving on the left side of the street. Ten years later, on April 18, 1922, vehicles switched to driving on the right side.

BY THE TIME THESE PHOTOS IN VICTORIA HARBOR WERE MADE IN 1912, the CPR's Empress Hotel (at left) had been open for just four years, and the British Columbia Parliament Buildings (far right) were still not completed, having been built in stages between 1893 and 1916. The Canadian Pacific Railway steamers had been making scheduled stops at Victoria for about ten years, using the Coast Steamship docks that are seen at right.

THE CANADIAN PACIFIC STEAMSHIPS, *PRINCESS ROYAL* AND *PRINCESS ADELAIDE*, were used on the Seattle-Vancouver–Victoria Triangle Route, and competed against the Puget Sound Navigation Co. steamer *Iroquois* until 1909. The 228-foot *Princess Royal*, 1,1997 tons, is at left. She was built of wood by the British Columbia Marine Railway Co. at Esquimalt, B.C. in 1907 and carried 750 first class passengers. She was the first CPR steamer to run the true Triangle Route, though she also made trips to Alaska. The *Princess Adelaide*, right, 3,061 tons, was built of steel by the Fairfield Yard in Glasgow, Scotland in 1910, and carried 240 first class and 1,200 day passengers. Fitted with a single triple expansion steam engine, she was slower than the CPR's two- and three-stackers, but much more economical. Though it appears a large pile of coal is on the dock, CPR was converting their steamers to burn oil at this time.

THE CANADIAN PACIFIC STEAMSHIP *PRINCESS MAY* was built for Formosa-Chinese mainland service by Hawthorne, Leslie and Co. of Newcastle England in 1888. Of 1394 tons, she ran under the names *Cass, Arthur, Cass* (again) *Ningchow,* and *Hating* before CPR purchased her in 1901. Operating in the Alaska trade, she was involved in a dramatic shipwreck on Alaska's Lynn Canal. Striking Sentinel Rock at full speed at high tide, August 5, 1910, she was left with 107 feet of her hull suspended over the rock. She was salvaged by expert Capt. W.H. Logan a month later.

THE STEAMSHIP *IROQUOIS* had a long history in the Pacific Northwest. The 1,169-ton ship, built in Ohio in 1901, was purchased by the Puget Sound Navigation Co. in 1906, along with the *Chippewa* and the *Indianapolis.* She steamed around Cape Horn the following year, and was placed on the Seattle–Victoria ferry run. In 1920 the *Iroquois* was sold and she returned to Great Lakes service. Seven years later she was repurchased by the Puget Sound Navigation Co., returned to the Pacific Northwest, and rebuilt, as shown here, to carry automobiles on the Seattle–Victoria run. Twenty years later the steamship was converted again, this time to a squat diesel freighter for the Seattle-Port Townsend-Port Angeles freight run. In 1973 she was rebuilt for use as a crab processor in Alaska.

THE THREE-STACK CANADIAN PACIFIC STEAMSHIP *PRINCESS ELAINE* was built at the John Brown Shipyard on the Clyde River in Scotland in 1928. Of 2,027 tons, she was a triple-screw turbine steamer. The vessel ran from Vancouver to Victoria, Nanaimo, Comox and the Gulf Islands. In 1963 she began her retirement serving as a restaurant ship at Blaine, Washington, and later Seattle. After a few idle years at the Sperry Dock at Tacoma, shown here, she was scrapped at Seattle in 1976.

THE FORMER TWIN-STACK CANADIAN PACIFIC STEAMER *PRINCESS MARGUERITE,* shown here under Stena Line ownership, is about to embark on her last voyage from Victoria to Seattle, September 9, 1989. Built by the Fairfield Co. in Glasgow Scotland, of 5,911 tons, she arrived at Esquimalt , near Victoria, B.C., on April l6, 1949. She was powered by twin screw, steam turbo-electric drive and made twenty-three knots. Put on the Seattle–Victoria– Vancouver Triangle Route, she could carry as many as 2,000 passengers. When the three-stack CPR steamer *Princess Elizabeth* was taken off the run in 1959, the *Princess Marguerite's* schedule was reduced to summer trips only, ending fifty-five years of continuous Seattle-Victoria service. She was kept on the Victoria–Vancouver run for one more year, then for the next twenty-nine years ran the Seattle–Victoria run in summer only. In 1972 a second automobile deck was added, nearly doubling her automobile capacity. The British Columbia Provincial Government took over her operation about 1972, until her sale to Stena Lines in 1988. She retired a year later, was reflagged Bahamian in 1991, and on February 20, 1992 left B.C. for Singapore in tow of the Russian tug *Rubin*. The plan to convert her to a hotel ship did not work out, and she was likely scrapped in Singapore in the late 1990s.

THE CANADIAN PACIFIC STEAMER, *PRINCESS PATRICIA,* sistership to the *Princess Marguerite,* arrived in Victoria in June of 1949, assisting on the Triangle Route until 1961 when she was used on the Vancouver–Nanaimo or Seattle–Victoria route. In 1963 she was converted to an Alaska cruise ship, as shown here, with accommodations for 347 passengers. As a cruise ship, she made eight to twelve voyages north each summer season, and for a time cruised between Los Angeles and Acapulco in the winter. She retired in 1981 and was used as a hotel ship at New Westminster, B.C. during Expo '86. In 1989 she went to Kaohsuing, Taiwan in tow of the tug *Baltic Rescuer* to be broken up.

A LONG BLAST ON THE *PRINCESS MARGUERITE'S* STEAM WHISTLE (left) marks her last scheduled departure from Victoria to Seattle on September 9, 1989.

THE IRON STEAMER *BREAKWATER,* A FORMER CARIBBEAN BANANA BOAT, ran on the Portland–San Francisco route for the Southern Pacific Railroad Co. and the North Pacific Steamship Co. prior to World War I.

THE STEAMER *BREAKWATER* always made a stop at Coos Bay, Oregon, to connect with the Southern Pacific Railroad line. Built in 1880 at Chester, Pennsylvania, of 1,065 tons, she made the Oregon–California run until she was sold Mexican in 1918.

THE SEATTLE WATERFRONT IN 1913 (overleaf) was dominated by numerous piers. The Smith Tower, which is shown here under construction, was built by typewriter magnate L.C. Smith. Completed in 1914, it stood as the tallest building west of the Mississippi until about 1967.

PASSENGERS POSE ON THE YACHT *WILMARTH* after a summer cruise on Elliott Bay. Seen in the background is the 293-ton *Waialeale*, built by the Hall Brothers in 1884. The steamer started her career in Hawaii but came to Puget Sound in 1902 and ran the Tacoma–Vancouver B.C. route. She was purchased by Puget Sound Navigation Co. in 1907 and served them for twenty years before being dismantled in Seattle. Note the little harbor launch *Tag* at right.

WITH CARGO BOOMS ON DECK, THE STEAM SCHOONER *A.G. LINDSAY*, (left) backs away from an Elliott Bay pier with a deckload of cargo bound for Alaska. Built at Detroit in 1899 for the Great Lakes ore trade, the 1,067 ton steamer was brought out to the Northwest for the West and Slade Wholesale Grocery Co. of Aberdeen in 1908. Soon thereafter she was chartered to the Alaska Navigation Co., and towed two barges and the sternwheel steamer *Julia B.*, 835 tons, to St. Michael for the Yukon Transportation Co. Later purchased by the Pacific American Fisheries Co. and renamed the *Pavlof*, she was lost on Trinity Island in 1915.

WHEN THE STEAMER *AKUTAN* RETURNED FROM THE ALEUTIAN ISLANDS in 1934 with a load of Alaskan furs, the entire crew was out on deck for their Seattle arrival. The *Akutan,* 266 tons, was built as a steam cannery tender by Kruse & Banks for the Alaska-Portland Packers Association and was fitted with a 350-hp compound engine. Tending the APPA Bristol Bay sailing gillnetter fleet until 1923, she was sold two years later to the Knappton Towboat Co. of Astoria, and became a freighter for Aleutian Island fur ranchers in the 1930s.

THE PACIFIC AMERICAN FISHERIES STEAMER *REDWOOD* (overleaf, left) was built at the PAF yard in Bellingham, along with the *Hollywood, Firwood, Rosewood,* in 1917 and *Oakwood,* in 1918. All were 1800 tons and fitted with twin screws and triple-expansion steam engines, producing 1,000-hp. Although the *Redwood* was held onto by PAF for eighteen years for Alaska fisheries work, the other steamers passed on to the Shipping Board. The *Redwood*, purchased by the Lowe Trading Co. (formerly the Associated Fisherman of Alaska) in 1935, was used for trading as far north as Nome, Wainwright, and Point Barrow, Alaska. In 1939 she was sold to Capt. Ajax Olsen and in 1941 was requisitioned by the U.S. Navy and used as a supply vessel.

THE STEAM SCHOONERS *CORNELIA, SIERRA* AND *DOROTHEA* (overleaf, right) await attention at Lake Union Dry Dock. The company, which has been in existence since 1919, and still repairs wooden ships, rebuilt a large portion of the *Virgina V's* hull in the late 1990s.

The steamer *Cornelia* had many names. Built in Oakland, California, in 1917 as the *Robert C. Sudden,* 1,430 tons, she was sold to French owners and renamed the *Hadrumette.* After World War I she came back to the Pacific Coast and was again named *Robert C. Sudden.* In the 1920s she was owned by Andy Mahony of San Francisco and her name was changed to *John C. Kirkpatrick.* About 1933 she was sold to the Northwestern Steamship Line, and used in the Puget Sound-Southeast Alaska trade, along with the wooden steamship *Evelyn Berg.* In 1935 she was sold to the Kitsap Lumber Co. of Tacoma, renamed the *Cornelia,* and returned to the coastwise lumber trade, but was laid up in 1937. After World War II she was purchased by the West Coast Steamship Co. and once again her name was changed, this time to the *West Coast.* She burned off Long Beach in 1946 and was then converted to a gypsum barge for use in Mexico.

The *Sierra,* of 1,510 tons, was the first of the traditional "steam schooners" to be powered by oil engines–two Bolinder 320-hp semi diesels–although she had a steam donkey boiler to power her anchor and cargo winches. Built at the Matthews Shipbuilding Co. at Hoquiam, Washington, for the Hart-Wood Lumber Co. in 1916, she had a lumber capacity of 1.25 million board feet. Damaged in a collision with the Matson liner *Wilhelmina* in 1923, she was sold to S.S. Freeman, and then sold four years later to the Arctic Transport Co. She was used, along with the *Silver Wave* and the *Donaldson,* for transporting reindeer meat until she was sold in 1936 for work as an Alaskan fish processor. During World War II she became a training ship at the Seattle Port of Embarkation, and then was assigned to the reserve fleet in Olympia. In 1948, she came back to Lake Union owned by Montana rancher William Studdert. Studdert later bought the schooner *Wawona* and in 1964 passed that historic ship on to John Ross and the organization "Save Our Ships." In 1966 the *Sierra* was sold to Mark Liikane and in 1975, in tow of the tug *Odin,* she returned to Grays Harbor. The plan was to restore her as a floating restaurant and maritime museum; however, she languished at Grays Harbor for a time and eventually wound up on a mudbank in the Chehalis River (see page 208.)

The *Dorothea,* of 116 tons, was built as a whaler at Seattle in 1910. After a fire she was rebuilt in Tacoma and a 100-hp Union Diesel was installed; however, she barely made seven knots. By the 1920s and 1930s, she was being used to transport supplies to the Aleutian Islands in all weather, and at all times. When she could not make progress against Bering Sea storms she would have to lay to, sometimes for days. Eventually a 200-hp diesel was installed, giving her a little more speed.

THE *ZR3*, THE *REDWOOD*, AND THE *INTERNATIONAL* are shown in layup on Seattle's Lake Union. The *ZR3* (left) was built as the *Muriel*, sistership to the *Donna Lane*, 2,200 tons, with two Skandia-Pacific diesel engines, by J.H. Price at Lake Washington Shipyard in 1920. Purchased by the Columbia River Smoked Fish Co. in 1925, she was later used as a herring processor in Alaska for the Atlantic and Pacific Packing Co. of New York. In 1932 Capt. J.C. Brownfield bought her for use as a freighter. Henry Emard of Seward, Alaska, purchased her in 1939, and after a series of layups in 1942 she was intentionally sunk to be part of a breakwater at Oyster Bay, near Vancouver, British Columbia. The *International* (right) was built as the Shipping Board steamer *Lake Singara* and in 1927 was converted to a floating cannery for use in Bristol Bay by the International Packing Co. of Seattle. She served in that capacity until 1940, when she was sold to East Coast interests. The wooden steamship *Redwood* (center) is mentioned on page 79.

THE STEAMSHIP *DAVID W. BRANCH,* shown here traversing the Ballard Locks in Seattle, was built in 1915 as the *Ecuador* for the Royal Dutch West Indies Mail Line by De Schelde Co. at Flushing, Netherlands. The *Branch* and two sisterships constructed along with her each carried about 110 first-class and 78 third-class passengers. Of 5,544 tons, she had a triple-expansion steam engine. In 1936 she was bought by Libby, McNeill and Libby to help in their Bristol Bay canning operation, and spent winter seasons in Seattle's Lake Union. She was taken over by the War Shipping Administration as a troop transport in 1941, and was sold to Greek owners after World War II.

THE ALASKA STEAMSHIP CO. was in business for seventy-seven years, from 1894 to 1971, starting out with the little steamer *Willapa* which departed Seattle for Alaska every two weeks. As the company grew over the years, it owned sixty-seven different ships, from the 146-ton *Oakland* to the 7,254-ton *Talkeetna*. The *Yukon*, at left, seen here loading passengers and freight at Pier 2, was purchased in 1924 for service to southwestern Alaska via the Inside Passage. Built in Philadelphia in 1899 as the *Havana*, 5,863 tons, she had twin screws powered by triple expansion steam engines of 5,000 hp. Like many Alaska Steam vessels, and other steamships of the time before the advent of such devices as radar and echo sounders, she had her share of mishaps—including a collision with the steamship *Columbia*, of the Alaska Line, at Jefferson Head, north of Port Madison, Washington. Her final voyage ended February 3,1946, with her grounding at the base of cliffs near Cape Fairfield in a severe winter storm, which prevented the removal of the 495 passengers and crew for forty-eight hours. When her stern section broke away and sank, forty-foot breaking seas swept twenty-one people off the deck and eleven were drowned. It is all but impossible to describe the force of breaking, forty-foot seas against a ship in this situation, and it was only through great acts of heroism that more people were not lost.

The *Alaska* was built in 1923 by Todd Shipyard to replace the original *Alaska*, of 1889 which was lost in 1921 when under charter to the San Francisco and Portland Steamship Co. The second *Alaska*, of 4,653 tons, had two triple-expansion steam engines developing a total of 5,600 hp. Repowered in 1931 with turbo-electrics, she made the Seattle-Ketchikan run in less than 40 hours. Alaska Steam discontinued passenger service in 1954, and the *Alaska* was sold a year later and renamed the *Mazatlan*.

THE *ADMIRAL FARRAGUT*, built in 1898 at Philadelphia, was originally ordered by the U.S. Navy, for the Spanish American War, along with three sister ships. Each was about 2,100 tons with two triple-expansion steam engines. The war ended before the ships were finished, and the *Farragut* was sold to the Boston Fruit Co. In 1912 the vessel was bought by H. F. Alexander's Pacific Alaskan Navigation Co., also known as the Admiral Line. When this photograph was made, in 1913, the *Farragut* was on scheduled runs along the Pacific Coast.

THE TWIN-STACK STEAMSHIP, *H.F. ALEXANDER*, right, flagship of the Admiral line, always had a reputation for great speed. She was built as the *Great Northern* by William Cramp and Sons of Philadelphia in 1914 for the Great Northern Pacific Steamship Co., and a year later arrived in Seattle along with the *Northern Pacific*. These sisterships, which accommodated 856 passengers each, were the finest liners of the day. Their twin Parson's turbine steam engines of 25,000 shaft hp could drive them at twenty-seven knots, although they consumed great quantities of fuel oil—about seventy-eight barrels an hour.

The U.S. Government used both vessels as troop carriers during World War I. In 1922 the Admiral Line purchased the *Northern Pacific*. However, upon taking possession of her, she caught fire and was destroyed, so they purchased the *Great Northern* (the ex-*Columbia*), and renamed her the *H.F Alexander*. She was used on the Seattle-San Francisco-Los Angeles run, and was very popular for the next ten years. In 1932, due to the Depression, she was sold to Robert Dollar and Co., along with the rest of the Admiral Line. The company operated under the name of Pacific Steamship Lines until 1936, when all coastwise passenger service south of Puget Sound ceased operations. In 1940 the *H.F Alexander* was sold to CPR, which operated her for the British Admiralty during the beginning of World War II. When the U.S. entered the war after the bombing of Pearl Harbor she was renamed *General George S. Simmonds* and was used as a U.S. transport. After the end of the war, although still in good condition, she was scrapped.

THE BRITISH-BUILT STEAMSHIP *HAIDA,* single-screw, 3,800 tons, built at Sunderland, England, in 1909, was typical of coal burning steamships of that era. When this photo was made on October 22, 1937, the *Haida,* under Chinese ownership but British flagged, had just taken on 5,000 tons of sulphur to be used in gunpowder manufacture for Chiang Kai-shek's fight against the Japanese. Soon after leaving Seattle on October 24 she disappeared; a life ring and oar were found three months later on a Vancouver Island beach—the only remains ever found.

THE *PACIFIC REDWOOD* AND THE *PACIFIC SPRUCE* in layup on Lake Union in the 1930's. Due to the Depression the 5,683 ton *Redwood* and the 5,509 ton *Spruce*, though only about twelve years old, sold for between $10,000 and $15,000 each in 1932.

THE W. R. GRACE CO. BUILT FOUR STEEL STEAMSHIPS in 1932 and 1933. The *Santa Rosa* was built by Federal Shipbuilding and Drydock of Kearney, New Jersey. She arrived at Seattle on December 18, 1932 for service to New York via San Francisco and Central and South America. Like her identical sisterships, the *Santa Paula*, *Santa Lucia*, and *Santa Elena*, she was driven by 12,000-hp steam turbines. The ship above is the *Santa Paula*. Service to the Northwest stopped in the fall of 1934.

THE AMERICAN MAIL LINE STEAMSHIP, *PRESIDENT MCKINLEY*, right, former Shipping Board (535 class) *Keystone State* of 1921, 14,127 tons was one of five such ships operated by the American Mail Line, between Puget Sound and the Orient. The others were named *President Grant*, *President Jefferson*, *President Madison*, (see page 204) and *President Jackson*. The *President McKinley* was fired upon in Shanghai in 1937 and was later restricted to freight service only, causing her to lose the government subsidy. She was laid up at Seattle in 1938, and is seen here taking on cargo at Pier 41. In 1940 the *President Madison* foundered off the coast of Japan while assisting another ship in distress. The other four Shipping Board liners were converted to World War II troopships later that year and were scrapped on the east coast in 1948.

THE PACIFIC AMERICAN FISHERIES STEAMSHIP *NORTH KING*, having made a slight navigation error in May of 1932, had no choice but to wait to be refloated by the next flood tide. She was built in Germany as the *Leibenfels* in 1903 and, starting in 1923, saw years of service for the Alaska-Portland Packers Association. In 1956 she was scrapped in Lisbon, Portugal.

THE STEAMSHIP *NORTH SEA*, right, the former Admiral Line steamer *Admiral Peoples*, was purchased for Alaska service in 1935 by Northland Transportation Co. Built in 1918 at Wilmington Delaware as the *Tipton*, 3,049 tons, she was single-screw and had a reciprocating steam engine of 1,700 hp. After many years of Alaska service she struck a reef near Bella Bella, British Columbia, on February 13, 1947. Although all 150 people aboard were saved, the steamer was not. This disaster ended the Northland Transportation Co., as their other steamers *Northland* and *North Coast* had previously been sold.

THE NORWEGIAN FREIGHTER *HARDANGER* OF BERGEN maneuvers into position for loading cargo at one of the Elliott Bay piers in Seattle. Traveling light, her propeller struggles to bite the water. This "whump, whump, whump" sound of the propeller is rarely heard anymore, due to water ballast systems so common today. Built at Port Glasgow, Scotland in 1924, 4,000 tons, the *Hardanger* participated in many World War II convoys.

THE MOTOR TANKER *ALEUTIAN NATIVE* built at Portland, Oregon, in 1913, 242 tons, started life as the Portland steam fireboat *David Campbell*, dousing fires there for fifteen years. In 1928 she was purchased by the Kanga Ranching Co., the largest fur rancher in the Aleutians, and was converted to haul freight to the Aleutian Islands. She joined the company's other trading schooners, the 67-foot *Iskum*, the 60-foot *Silver Wave*, the 106-foot *Dorothea* (see pages 79–81), the 110-foot *Maid of Orleans,* and the 87-foot *Einar Beyer* (later *Robert M*). In 1932 the *Aleutian Native* was purchased by the newly-formed Petroleum Navigation Co. and was converted to an oil tanker. She is shown above, in PNC colors, and dressed for Maritime Day festivities in Seattle. Eight years later the company purchased another, larger 469-ton tanker and renamed it the *Dispatch* and renamed the *Aleutian Native* the *Express* at the same time. In the late 1950s she was sold to the Upper Columbia River Towing Co., and converted to a tug.

TAKING ON CARGO AT THE AMERICAN MAIL LINE PIER, the *Aleutian Native* prepares for her departure.

THE MOTORSHIP *FRANCIS BARKLEY*, works on the Port Alberni–Barkley Sound Route today. Built in Stavanger, Norway, of 297 tons, she worked there until her purchase by Alberni Marine Transportation, Ltd. in 1990. She sailed to Port Alberni via the Panama Canal from June 20 to August 11, 1990. She works out of Port Alberni, still powered by her original Bergen diesel, making 400 hp at 450 rpm.

THE MOTORSHIP *LADY ROSE*, was built on the Clyde River, Scotland, 199 tons, of riveted steel like the larger CPR steamers. She was originally fitted with the first National diesel built, producing 220 hp. Today she has a six-cylinder Caterpillar engine producing 385 hp at 850 rpm. Originally named *Lady Sylvia*, she left Scotland May 7, 1937, and arrived in Vancouver, B.C. on July 11. She worked Howe Sound for the Union Steamship Company, and later worked for Coast Ferries, Ltd. in the Gulf Islands. In 1960 she ran the Port Alberni–Barkley Sound route, and continues to haul freight and passengers on the route today. Her voyage across the Atlantic was so rough that the crew kept the lavatory sinks packed with oil and oakum. The oil dripped out to calm the seas.

THE COASTAL MOTOR TANKER *GENERAL*, idles along under Seattle's Fremont Bridge. Built in San Francisco in 1926, of 570 tons, the *General* was owned by General Petroleum Co. of California. In the 1950s Puget Sound Tug and Barge used her as a barge, then sold her to Mariner Steamship Co. of Baltimore in 1956. She steamed to Baltimore under her own power.

SHIPYARDS LIKE THE LAKE UNION DRY DOCK AND MACHINE WORKS (right) were most important to the economy of the Pacific Northwest. This shipyard, founded In 1919 by John McLean and Otis Cutting on the southeast shore of Lake Union, built a wide range of vessels over the years, from the first large tuna clipper, the 126-foot *Espirito Santo*, built in 1934, to the 75-foot U.S. Patrol Boat *No. 263*, built in 1924. This latter vessel was the first of fifteen rum-chasers built with enough speed to compete with the ingenuity of the Northwest rum-runners. The shipyard was perhaps most notable for its construction of the L.E. (Ted) Geary-designed yachts. John McLean, president of Lake Union Dry Dock formed Associated Shipbuilders in 1940 with H.W. McCurdy, president of Puget Sound Bridge and Dredging Co. At the time PSB&D had fewer resources for finishing vessels, so the original plan was for hulls to be constructed at PSG docks, and completed at Lake Union Dry Dock. This joint venture, not working smoothly, was ended after McLean's death in 1944. In the photo, the yacht *Marilyn III* (center) has just been launched, and the Ted Geary-designed yacht *Stranger* is being built at left The retired lightship in the background is possibly the *Umatilla Reef* of 1897. The steamer next to the lightship is possibly the *Mohawk*.

THE MOTORSHIP *DONNA LANE*, 2,200 tons, above and right, at Lake Union Drydock, was built in 1920 by the J.H. Price Construction Co., Houghton, Washington, and was powered by twin 6-cylinder, 500 hp MacIntosh and Seymour diesels. In early 1926 she was purchased by I.C. Jacobsen of Seattle, and in 1927 she was sent to the Prince William Sound-Cook Inlet region of Alaska. There she operated as the first Alaskan ship prepared to freeze fish, and was capable of freezing 50 tons of fish a day. In 1941 she was sold to the Marine Export Co. of New York who then passed her on to the Flomarcy Co. of Rio de Janeiro.

THE *DONNA LANE* IS SHOWN ON ONE OF LAKE UNION DRYDOCK'S wooden floating drydocks for annual maintenance. These drydocks are flooded with water, causing them to submerge enough to allow a ship to float on top of their deck. High capacity pumps then remove the water from the drydock hull raising it, and the ship along with it.

A MACHINIST checks out ring and pinion gears on the anchor windlass of the *Donna Lane,* which can be one of the most stressed machines on a ship. Shafts and gearing can become misaligned as the fo'c'sle head of a wooden ship settles over time.

LAKE UNION DRYDOCK shipwrights remove the shaft and propeller of the steam tug *Humaconna* (right).

HOUGHTON, LOCATED JUST SOUTH OF KIRKLAND on Lake Washington's east side, with its gently sloping sandy beaches, lent itself to the simpler boat building techniques of the late nineteenth century. After the boats were constructed the builders would wait until flood season to launch them. One of the pioneer boats built on the beach was the steam-powered *Squak*, of 1884. In 1901 George Bartsch and H.E. Tompkins opened a small shipyard at Houghton—the start of the Lake Washington Shipyard. Around 1908 Capt. John L. Anderson took over management of the yard; the first to be built under Anderson was the 87-ton steamer *Atlanta*, for his own use.

About 1914, Anderson moved the entire shipyard to an abandoned mill site close to the Elliott Bay sawmill on Seattle's waterfront in order to build the 313-ton steel steamer *Bainbridge*. It was launched into saltwater in 1915. When the Government Locks and Lake Washington Ship Canal opened, Anderson moved his operations back to Houghton, but in 1918 he sold the yard to E.H. Price of Portland, who finished Anderson's contracts for the wooden motorships *Muriel (ZR3)*, and the *Donna Lane*.

THE STEEL STEAMSHIP *W.M. TUPPER* ON LAKE WASHINGTON SHIPYARD'S railway joins a wooden power schooner for repairs in 1934. The *W.M. Tupper* was built in 1917 in Jacksonville, Florida, of 1,756 tons, and was owned by the Santa Ana Steamship Company, and used for Arctic trading. She made regular calls at Bristol Bay and the Kuskokwim River.

THE CANNERY TENDER *BOHEMIA*, being built at Jim Warren's Boathouse and Marine Ways, is being checked out by H.E. "Jamie" Jamiesen, marine reporter for the Seattle Star, on the right, and the lead shipwright on the project, at left.

THE *BOHEMIA'S* DECKHOUSE BEGINS TO TAKE SHAPE at Jim Warren's, on the Duwamish River. Note the canvas army duck covering the big thickness planer and railway winch. Coverings like this were not uncommon for an open air shipyard of this type. The *Bohemia*, 74 tons, was built for Hanson Transportation Co. and launched in 1940.

BELLINGHAM MARINE WAYS (later Bellingham Shipyards), located just north of what is now Squalicum Harbor, was busy with tug and fishboat construction and repair. In 1951 it was awarded a government contract to build five 165-foot minesweepers. A smaller shipyard still exists near this location today. Note Clift Motor Co., a builder of marine engines, and the web shed at right.

THE JOINER SHOP AT BELLINGHAM MARINE WAYS shows a typical setup in shipyards built before World War II, with all machinery driven by flat belts turning on various jack shafts driven by one power source.

PUGET SOUND BRIDGE AND DREDGING CO. had its beginnings in San Francisco, in 1886. That same year John McCullen started his carpentry business. He later joined engineers George W. Catt and Herman Krusi and formed the San Francisco Bridge Co. The Seattle office was established March 31, 1889, and became an independent business in 1905. Over the years the company has been involved with projects such as building dams, bridges, and ships. They moved over twenty-five million yards of dredged material to construct one of the world's largest man-made islands, Harbor Island, at the mouth of Seattle's Duwamish River where the company was located. The photo above shows warehouses and dredge pipe at Plant One, on the West Waterway.

THE HYDRAULIC DREDGE, *PORT TOWNSEND*, like all their equipment, was designed and built by PSB&D. This is a view of the cutterhead, which used sixteen-inch pipe to move the spoils. Dipper and hoe dredges like the *Seattle 4* used (dumping) barges. It was convenient to have Standard Boiler Works nearby, as most of the ships and dredges PSB&D built in their early years were steam powered.

THE *SEATTLE 4,* SEEN HERE IN TOW OF THE *ARTHUR FOSS,* was typical of the hoe dipper dredges used in later years. The *Seattle 4* was towed to the upper Columbia River, where she did a substantial amount of dredging. H.W. McCurdy joined PSB&D in 1922 and became president of the company in 1929. He retired in 1959 when Lockheed Aircraft Corp. purchased the shipbuilding and construction company in June of that year. Lockheed ran the operation for about thirty years, but liquidated it in 1989. Puget Sound Dredging was kept as a separate business until 1975, when H.W. "Mac" McCurdy again retired. His son, J.G. McCurdy, joined the business after World War II, in 1947, and later became president of Puget Sound Bridge and Dry Dock.

THE CUTTERHEAD, shown here on the far right, is the business end of a hydraulic dredge operation. Note the skiff of the U.S. Engineering Department tied to the scow, probably to help keep track of various operations

THE STEAM-POWERED PILE DRIVER OF THE HART CONSTRUCTION CO. adds piling to a dock near Fox Island on south Puget Sound. Steam is let off to the atmosphere whenever the main hoist is operating (above), as the boilers are non-condensing. The tug in the background is possibly the *Sam Foss*.

THE STEEL PIPE HELD BY THE WORKER (right) was used to shoot water at the location of the piling to be driven, to loosen up the seabed. Hart Construction Co. had offices in Tacoma and Longview; in the mid-1970s it was bought by General Construction Co., which still is in operation today. This is a "moonraker" style pile driver, which allows the driver to install pile at an angle.

BUILDING A SYSTEM OF LOCKS AND A SHIP CANAL linking Puget Sound to Lake Washington was first brought up by Gen. George B. McClellan in 1853 while he was doing railroad survey work in Salmon Bay. Early Seattle settler Thomas Mercer then mentioned the prospect of a canal in 1854, in a Fourth of July speech. The project began when a fellow named Henry Pike was so taken by the idea of cutting a canal, in order to facilitate the transport of logs and coal from Lake Washington to Puget Sound, that in 1860 he filed for a 200-foot-wide tract of land in what is now the Montlake area, and with pick and shovel began digging the canal by himself. After coming to the conclusion that he couldn't dig the canal single-handedly, he formed the Lake Washington Canal Association which filed for government assistance in 1871.

That same year the Army Corps of Engineers sent out Gen. Barton S. Alexander to survey the area and estimate the cost of the project. The U.S. War Department was looking for a naval station site for ship repairing and resupplying. If Lake Washington could be connected to Puget Sound, it would be a prime candidate. Alexander came up with three possible routes for a canal, and an estimate of four million dollars to build it. At the time Congress thought the cost was too high, so Bremerton was selected for the naval station instead, and government support of the project was dropped.

However, local appetites were whetted by the potential commercial value of the canal. In 1894 Congress authorized funds to deepen Salmon Bay, thus making this route the most feasible. A route different from the one the War Department initially preferred was surveyed, and costs for this canal were estimated at $2.9 million. A right-of-way was donated by King County in 1900. Construction did not begin until 1911, and by then the cost estimate had risen to $8 million, due to a stronger economy after the 1895 depression, and some aggressive land speculation that had occurred. Under the direction of Maj. Hiram M. Chittenden of the Army Corps of Engineers, work was completed on the locks in July 1916 and they

of Maj. Hiram M. Chittenden of the Army Corps of Engineers, work was completed on the locks in July 1916 and they began operation. Over 16,000 vessels used them the first year. On the Fourth of July, 1917, sixty-three years after Thomas Mercer's speech, an official opening ceremony was held, with the *Roosevelt* the first vessel to officially pass through the locks.

The locks, located in Seattle's Ballard district, are referred to by various names including the Ballard Locks, the Government Locks, and the Hiram M. Chittenden Locks (the official title). The two canals that connect it to Lake Washington are known as the Lake Washington Ship Canal and the Montlake Cut.

In the photo at left, note the track laid for railcars to remove material. The photo at the bottom, above, shows dirt used as ballast on the coffer dam.

HURRICANE-FORCE WINDS struck western Washington on October 21, 1934. Seventeen people were killed by the storm and hundreds were injured. Five of the dead were crewmen aboard the seiner *Agnes*, which foundered in the Strait of Juan de Fuca off Point Wilson. On Puget Sound, numerous vessels were torn from their moorings and huge trees were uprooted; buildings had roofs ripped off, walls collapsed, and windows broken. Logs and debris loosed by the storm acted as battering rams, inflicting damage on vessels and buildings along the shores. On Lake Union, a loose log boom raced the length of the lake in just minutes, threatening houseboats, and eventually grounding on the lake's north shore at the gas plant.

The American Mail liner *President Madison*, which had been tied fore and aft across the south end of Pier 41 in Smith Cove, snapped her mooring lines, and with winds up to eighty mph pushing her broadside toward the shore, she drifted the length of Pier 41. The huge liner ripped three other vessels loose and swept them along with her, piling them up against tugs and barges moored at the end of the pier. The steamboat *Harvester* was sunk; however, her crew of twenty scrambled to safety. The tug *Roosevelt* and several barges and smaller tugs were damaged, and pilings and planking on Piers 40 and 41 were scraped loose by the bow and stern of the liner. The *President Madison* herself sustained only minor damage.

BROWN'S BOATHOUSE AT LESCHI suffered damage and many boats were lost or damaged in the 1934 storm. Peter Leplant lived here and built boats on the site until about 1924.

THE MOSQUITO FLEET STEAMER *VIRGINIA V*, AT LAKE UNION DRYDOCK, (overleaf) was a casualty of the violent storm of October 21, 1934. She suffered extensive damage when coming alongside the Ollala dock. A gust of wind estimated at over seventy knots heeled the steamer over against the dock with such impact that several pilings were broken. The shattered pilings pierced her topsides and pinned her against the dock. Passengers and crew were able to escape to the pier, but the ships's starboard side was stove in, the upper decks collapsed, and the pilot house sagged to the level of the main deck. Note the steam schooner in the background and the U.S.R.C. *Snohomish* at the left, in front of the steam plant.

THE OWNERS OF THE VIRGINIA V, the West Pass Transportation Co., decided to rebuild immediately. The steamer, seen here at the Lake Union Dry Dock for an initial survey, was towed to Lake Washington Shipyard at Houghton, stripped down to its main deck and rebuilt in just a few weeks. Note the steam schooner in the background.

CAPT. NELS G. CHRISTENSEN SURVEYS A SAD SIGHT TO BEHOLD, the wreck of the finest vessel ever to run on the West Pass. The $11,000 reconstruction of the *Virginia V* was completed on December 5, 1934, causing her to be out of operation only about six weeks. The Christensen family's decision to rebuild at a time when most other steamers were being scrapped, enabled her to survive to this day.

AT THE SAME TIME THE *VIRGINIA V* WAS REBUILT, the ferry *Peralta* (top) was being rebuilt into the streamlined *Kalakala*. The *Kalakala* was completed in July of 1935.

THE *VIRGINIA V* HULL WAS NOT DAMAGED by the storm, nor was most of the machinery, including the Barlow marine elevator. The elevator, which saved time transferring freight, generally was run by the fireman and was powered by a Stanley Steamer automobile engine. Note the engine room gauges and framed sign that reads: "Safety first. Take no chances." The triple-expansion engine was actually built for the U.S. Government by Heffernan Engine Works of Seattle in 1898, and had been used in the *Virginia IV* (ex-*Tyrus*), of 1904. This engine produced 400 hp at 200 rpm at 175 psi. (see page 192) The Roberts-type water tube boiler in the right of the picture, was constructed by H.S. Studdert of Seattle and burned bunker C fuel oil.

THE *VIRGINIA V* IS SHOWN HERE BEFORE HER 1934 REBUILD. She was built by master shipwright "Big Timber" Matt Anderson for Captain Nels G. Christensen, and his sons Captains Nels C., Vern, and Andrew, owners of the West Pass Transportation Co. She was constructed between 1921 and 1922, at Maplewood, on the Kitsap Peninsula, of 3-inch fir planking over 8 x 8-inch fir frames. Her hull measured 125 feet in length, with a 24-foot beam, and 11-foot maximum draft.

THE *VIRGINIA V*, SEEN HERE RIGHT AFTER HER REBUILD, was basically a new vessel from her main deck up. The more commodious wheelhouse and cabin are the most noticeable differences. The Christensen family held out as long as possible, but with declining revenues they could no longer turn a profit, and the vessel made her last West Pass run in 1939. During World War II she ran the Fort Worden–Seattle route, for a short time worked the Portland–Astoria route on the Columbia River, and then worked in the San Juan Islands between 1944 and 1954. Puget Sound Excursion Lines used her until about 1968, then after a few close calls she was recognized as a National Historic Site in 1973. The *Virginia V* Foundation was formed in 1976 to preserve this sole survivor of a colorful period of Puget Sound's history. In the late 1990s she is undergoing a major restoration of hull and machinery.

THE STEAMER *MONTICELLO,* SEEN HERE IN EARLY 1936 just prior to her conversion to a diesel freighter, serves as a convenient billboard for striking unions. Built in 1906 at the Crawford and Reid yard at Tacoma, of 196 tons, the *Monticello* was fitted with a triple-expansion steam engine, working at 250 lbs pressure. She ran the Seattle–Poulsbo route, and later the Seattle–Port Blakely run. In 1936, renamed *Penaco,* she carried freight on Puget Sound routes. She was later used for crab fishing in Alaska and renamed *Sea Venture*; the vessel foundered off the Aleutian Islands in 1962.

The Pacific Coast Longshore unions went on strike May 9, 1934. They were soon joined by the Seamens, Firemens, Cooks, and Stewards unions and Masters, Mates, and Pilots Association, effectively shutting down all West Coast ports. Strikes continued on and on through the 1930s, with the unions wanting an eight-hour work day, six-day work week, and a livable wage. Although the Inland Boatmen's Union had a six-day work week agreement then, and the inland fleets kept steaming in 1934, they struck in 1936 (photo above). The strikes were the final blow to many historic coastwise steamship lines that were barely hanging on during the Depression.

THE STEAMER *VASHONA* AT COLMAN DOCK, AND THE FIREBOAT *ALKI* at her station (see page 187), lie near the Colman Dock in wait of a job. The *Vashona* was one of only two passenger steamers built after 1920 on Puget Sound. Of 185 tons, she was built by John Martinolich at Dockton in 1921 for the Vashon Navigation Co.'s Tacoma–Vashon Island route. In 1926 her original steam engine was replaced with the *Utopia's* triple-expansion engine from 1893.

Due to the lack of passenger traffic the *Vashona* was replaced by the smaller *Concordia* and was taken off the Tacoma route. She was sold to Anderson Steamboat Co. for use in their excursion service, and renamed *Sightseer*. In 1946 Anderson passed the *Sightseer* on to Grayline Tours of Seattle who put her on the Lake Washington Ship Canal–Puget Sound run. In 1963 she was replaced by the *Holiday,* which was renamed *Sightseer*, and the original *Sightseer* was again renamed, this time as *Columbia Queen* when she was sold for Columbia River excursion service. By the late 1960s the former *Vashona* was languishing near Pasco, Washington; finding no buyers at $500, she was abandoned on the riverbank about 1969.

THE *SIGHTSEER* TRAVERSES THE BALLARD LOCKS in 1938 (overleaf).

THE STEAMER *VERONA*, 142 tons, was built by the Martinolich Bros. at Dockton, in 1910 for the Vashon Navigation Co. and equipped with a triple-expansion steam engine. She ran on the Tacoma–Quartermaster Harbor route. The *Verona* was probably most famous for her role as the "Wobbly Battleship" in 1916 when on the Seattle-Everett run. Boarded by members of the I.W.W. for a planned demonstration at Everett, gunfire ensued during landing. By the time she left minutes later, seven people were left dead, forty-seven wounded, and two to twelve drowned from falling in the water.

The *Verona* was owned by the Kitsap County Transportation Co. after 1923, and was used on the Fauntleroy–Vashon and Seattle–Bainbridge run during the 1930s. She caught fire at Seattle in 1936, and was destroyed.

THE STEAMER *ATALANTA* laid up at the Lake Washington Shipyard.

MOSQUITO FLEET STEAMERS ARE LAID UP AT LAKE WASHINGTON SHIPYARD in 1937 (overleaf).

FACING AN UNCERTAIN FUTURE, THE PUGET SOUND MOSQUITO FLEET LIES IN WAIT at the Lake Washington Shipyard, near Houghton (present day Kirkland). Except for the *Virgina V*, not one of these vessels survives today.

The term "Mosquito Fleet" was the name commonly (and affectionately) used during the 1920s for the vessels that linked communities along Puget Sound. These several hundred ships, most of them small steamers, were so numerous and so active that they resembled a swarm of mosquitoes. Early communities developed along the shore, since land connections were primitive roads–if there were roads at all. Boats were the primary communication link between these communities, with the whistle of the steamer summoning townsfolk to the wharf. Mail contracts were a vital part of a boat's success. With a contract in hand for carrying mail to particular communities, a steamboat or shipping line was assured of steady income for a while. Competition was stiff, especially in early times, and vessels often did multiple duty, carrying passengers, mail, freight, livestock, and towing logs–occasionally all at the same time. The steamers ranged from bare-bones to palatial, and also served as recreation, carrying passengers on sightseeing trips or excursions to welcome visiting dignitaries, large ships, and other significant visitors.

EARLY STEAMERS were either propeller driven or sidewheelers, although sternwheelers became popular later. Because of the varied quality of the coal or wood fuel, boilers could be temperamental and subject to overheating, and explosions were not infrequent. Except for a few notable disasters, the occasional explosion or wreck yielded surprisingly few fatalities. This might have been due to the fact that there were so many boats around to assist and pick up survivors.

Speed was essential to the profitable operation of the Mosquito Fleet steamers, and therefore races between the speedier ships were important. Sometimes these were impromptu races that occurred when two rivals met, headed for the same destination, and passengers found themselves partaking of the competition. It was not uncommon for the passengers themselves to urge the race. Other times races were staged events on a predetermined course, with spectators on shore or in nearby steamers cheering on their favorite. Winner of the race was awarded a gilded broom, which was attached to the stack, indicating they had swept the competition.

The steamships were able to compete financially with the railroad when it arrived; however, the advent of automobiles and trucks along with good roads signaled a new type of fast, inexpensive travel that the steamers were unable to meet. This brought about the demise of the fleet. A contributing factor was labor disputes, strikes, and boycotts that affected shipping for periods during the 1930s, and caused financial problems for boat owners. The era of the Mosquito Fleet was over by World War II, and many aging steamers were scrapped then, and the metal was recycled for ammunition and war materials. Other ships of the Mosquito Fleet became fish processors or saw other service in Alaska.

PACIFIC NORTHWEST FERRIES REPLACED THE MOSQUITO FLEET. The
steamship *Chippewa* arrived at Seattle in 1906, along with two other Great Lakes steamers, the *Indianapolis* and the *Iroquois,*
purchased by the Puget Sound Navigation Co. The *Chippewa*, of 887 tons, which was built at Toledo, Ohio, in 1900 was used
on the Seattle–Victoria run, and later the Seattle–Tacoma route. After service as a training ship for the Shipping Board
during World War I, along with the *Iroquois*, she was sold to the Chicago and South Haven Steamship Co. and returned to
Great Lakes service. Five years later the vessel returned to Puget Sound Navigation Co. ownership. In 1926 she was
converted to a car ferry at Lake Washington Shipyard, becoming the largest on Puget Sound and carrying up to 2,000
passengers and 90 automobiles on the Seattle–Bremerton run. Eight years later she underwent another major rebuild; this
time her steam engine was replaced with an eight cylinder, 2,200 hp Busch-Selzer diesel and one stack was removed (as
shown here), which gave her a more modern look. She remained a car ferry until 1964, when she was sold to the Foss
Launch and Tug Co. for use as a floating warehouse.

THE *CHETZEMOKA* AND *SAN MATEO* are seen laid up at Eagle Harbor in September of 1969. Built in 1927 at Alameda, California, as the diesel-electric *Golden Poppy,* 779 tons, the *Chetzemoka* arrived in Washington from San Francisco in 1938 and was renamed after a well-known Klallam Indian chief from the Port Townsend area who was a friend of the local settlers. She was owned by the County Transportation Co. and was used on the Fauntleroy–Vashon and Seattle–Bainbridge runs during the 1930s. Washington State Ferries sold her to California interests about 1975; however, while heading south in tow of the *Express,* she foundered off Cape Flattery.

A FERRY GALLEY, 1935. Soup was ten cents, chili fifteen cents, and you could always get a hot cup of coffee.

RIDING A FERRY IN 1933 was great fun for a family, just as it is today. This group is aboard the wooden ferry *Vashon*, 641 tons, built at Lake Washington Shipyard in 1930, with an eight cylinder Washington-Estep diesel. The *Vashon* provided fifty years of service on nearly all ferry routes, including the San Juan Islands. An effort in 1981 to preserve this last operating wooden Northwest ferry did not generate enough interest, so she was sold to become a fish processor. However, she ran aground soon after arriving in southeast Alaska.

TWO RETIRED FERRIES, THE *SKANSONIA* AND THE *KALAKALA,* are lucky to be afloat today, and unlike most retired vessels of their size, have patrons interested in their preservation. The *Skansonia,* of 446 tons, was built in 1929 at Gig Harbor by the Skansie Dry Dock and Shipbuilding Co. She could carry sixty-five automobiles and five hundred passengers. Owned by William Skansie's Washington Navigation Co., the ferry worked the Point Defiance–Gig Harbor route until the construction of the Tacoma Narrows Bridge in 1940. However, when the bridge collapsed just four months later the *Skansonia,* along with the *City of Tacoma* and the *Defiance,* resumed service until the new suspension bridge was finished ten years later. The *Skansonia* then continued service between Tacoma and Vashon Island for Washington State Ferries until she was replaced by the *Hiyu* which was built at Portland in 1967. Today the *Skansonia* is a restaurant-banquet ship on Seattle's Lake Union.

The streamlined *Kalakala,* the "Flying Bird," began her career as the steam ferry *Peralta.* Built by Moore Dry Dock Co. at Oakland in 1927, of 2,000 tons, she operated on the Key Transit Co.'s San Francisco–Oakland route. In 1933 the *Peralta* was severely burned by a fire that broke out in the terminal where it was moored. That September Capt. Alexander Peabody of the Puget Sound Navigation Co., purchased the damaged vessel for $18,000 with the idea of rebuilding it, and the tug *Creole* towed it to Seattle.

The modernized ferry was conceived by Capt. Peabody and designed by Boeing engineer Louis Procter. The superstructure was built by Lake Washington Shipyard in Houghton, utilizing their newly invented electric arc welder, and was overseen by James Murphy and Frederick Wilhelm Helmuth "Bull" Schmitz. (see page 126). With a new 3,000 hp Busch-Sulzer diesel installed, she made her maiden voyage to Bremerton on July 2, 1935 (photo at right), skippered by Capt. Wallace Mangan and escorted by the steamer *Tacoma* carrying reporters and cameramen. The art-deco ferry received world-wide attention, and trips aboard her were immensely popular. In the early years a special cruise every evening featured dancing to the Flying Bird Orchestra. The forward cabin was cleared of chairs to provide a dance floor.

THE *KALAKALA* HEADS TOWARD RICH PASSAGE IN 1935. During World War II the *Kalakala* saw heavy duty, daily carrying thousands of shipyard workers and servicemen across Puget Sound to the Bremerton navy yards. After the end of the war she received the first of the declassified commercial radar unit developed by wartime technology.

When Washington State took over the operation of the ferry system and bought the *Kalakala*, along with other vessels of the Puget Sound Navigation Co. (Black Ball Line), the ferry was assigned to the Port Angeles–Victoria run. A larger, five-blade propeller, which replaced the old propeller in 1956, was effective in significantly reducing the serious vibrations that had plagued the ferry since its redesign. In 1960 the Black Ball Line took over the Port Angeles–Victoria ferry route from the state, replacing the *Kalakala* with the new *Coho*, which is still in service today. The state ferry was returned to service on the Bremerton route, and during the 1962 Seattle World's Fair was voted the area's second biggest attraction, after the Space Needle.

After thirty-two years of service on Washington waters, the *Kalakala* made her last run on October 2, 1967. She was sold to American Freezer Ships and towed to Dutch Harbor, Alaska to be converted to a crab and shrimp processor. In 1969 she was moved up on the beach at Gibson Cove, in Kodiak, Alaska, to serve as a land-based shrimp processor. It was thought she would never see the water again.

However, Seattleite Peter Bevis, remembering the vessel's glory days, became determined to resurrect and restore her. In 1998 Bevis and friends, overcoming incredible odds, refloated the *Kalakala* and moved her to navigable water. In October of that year, in tow of the tug *Neptune* and a little worse for wear, she reached Seattle. As of 1999 she is moored on Lake Union, undergoing restoration. Plans are for her to become a permanent waterfront attraction, housing a museum and shops.

THE STEAM FERRY *SAN MATEO*, SEEN HERE MOORED ON THE FRASER RIVER IN 1999, was one of only three San Francisco ferries, of many to come to Puget Sound, to keep her name. Of 1,780 tons, and built of steel by the Union Iron Works of San Francisco in 1922, she and her two sister ships, *Shasta* and *Yosemite,* were powered by World War I surplus triple-expansion steam engines (from the Ferris-type wood cargo ships built for the Shipping Board). Owned by the Southern Pacific-Golden Gate Ferry Co. in the 1920s and 1930s, she contained fifty tons of railcar brakeshoes for ballast, courtesy of the Southern Pacific Railway.

The *San Mateo* was the last of the steam-powered ferries to operate on Puget Sound. The 229-foot vessel was one of a fleet of six similar double-ended ferries that were operated on San Francisco Bay by the Southern Pacific–Golden Gate Ferry Co. The completion of the Bay Area bridges brought an end to the San Francisco ferry system. The *San Mateo* and her sister ship, the *Shasta*, were purchased by the Puget Sound Navigation Co. in 1940, two of many that made the transition from San Francisco to meet the growing demand for automobile ferries on Puget Sound.

The *San Mateo* and *Shasta* were part of the fleet bought by the state when it took over the operation of ferries in 1951. Because steamships required more manpower to operate than diesel vessels, and since the *San Mateo* held only 650 passengers and about fifty-five cars, she was costly to run. By the late 1960s the aging steam ferry was used only on a reserve basis, primarily on the Seattle–Winslow run, and in September, 1969 she was permanently retired and laid-up in Bainbridge Island's Eagle Harbor. The *Shasta*, which had been sold off earlier, became a floating restaurant on Portland's Willamette River .

THE *SAN MATEO'S* GALLEY AND ENGINE ROOM today are very much as they appeared in 1922, although all glass is missing, including the stained glass of the upper deckhouse windows. The 1,400-hp triple-expansion steam engine (right) looks as if it could run tomorrow; however, the three water tube boilers might need some attention before producing any steam pressure.

In recognition of her steam engine, design, and place in West Coast history, the ferry, with her high, graceful stack, mahogany woodwork, and stained-glass saloon windows, was listed on the National Register of Historic Places in 1971, making federal funds available for repair work. In August of 1971 the vessel was purchased by Washington State Parks for $20,000; the state, working in conjunction with the City of Seattle and historic groups, planned to restore her and maintain her as a historic site. Restoration of roofing, electrical work, decks, gangways, and fire protection would cost an estimated $100,000. However, the steamer was in worse shape than anticipated. After sinking $200,000 into repairs, and with at least another $500,000 in the offing, the state decided to drop the project in 1975, considering it too expensive.

A private non-profit group, the Historic Seattle Preservation and Development Authority, took over the renovation, and in 1978 moved the *San Mateo* from the Seattle waterfront to Lake Union. For years she was moored at the Naval Reserve pier on Lake Union, but it was determined that she was more than they could handle at the time. About 1993 she found new patrons in Garry and Dee Bereska, who towed her a few miles up the Fraser River and hope to restore her soon. Her 47-foot stack was removed so it wouldn't fall on its own accord.

PUGET SOUND FREIGHT LINES HAS A LONG HISTORY in the Pacific Northwest.

The company dates from 1919, when Capt. Frank E. Lovejoy leased, and later bought, the little gas freight boat *Chaco*, replacing her cranky gas engine with a semi-diesel. With business picking up on his Seattle-Tacoma-Olympia route, in 1921 he asked John Martinolich at Dockton to build another vessel for him, the 65 foot *Rubaiyat*, of 66 tons. However, two years later Martinolich built another freight boat, the *Capitol*, 148 tons, to replace the *Rubaiyat*. The vessel capsized with the loss of four crew members; although it was a calm day, the topside freight doors had been left open and the wake of the passing steamer *Indianapolis* caused water to enter the hull. She was later salvaged and towed to Port Blakely, where she was rebuilt into the little motor ferry *City of Kingston* . By 1926 Capt. Lovejoy needed more vessels, and he purchased the sternwheeler *S.G.Simpson* and the diesel freighter *Seal*. In 1929 PSFL bought Merchants Transportation Co. The purchase included the newly built *Belana* , of 244 tons, (above), the *Seatac*, (see page 204), the *F.H. Marvin*, the *V.P. Handy*, and the *A.W.Sterrett*.

THE GRAND TRUNK PACIFIC DOCK, which later became Canadian National Pier 53, was the PSFL terminal at Seattle until the mid-1950s. Shown here are the freight boats *Chimacum* and *Capitol*, and the steamer *Mohawk*, at right. The *Mohawk* was built as the twin-screw motor passenger vessel *Islander* by Albert Jensen at Friday Harbor, Washington in 1921, 220 tons, for the Seattle–San Juan run of the Island Transportation Co. She was rebuilt into the single-screw steamer *Mohawk* in 1927 for carrying passengers and freight. The *Chimacum* of 110 tons, was built in 1928, and was purchased from J.K. Munson and Sons and worked for PSFL until the steamer's sale to the Horluck Transportation Co. of Port Orchard in 1943.

THE 65-FOOT DIESEL FREIGHTER, *CAPITOL*, 148 tons, was built in 1924 by John Martinolich at Dockton, Washington. The *Rubaiyat* had just capsized and the *Chaco* had caught fire and burned to the waterline near Point Defiance, so the *Capitol* arrived none too soon. She was larger than the company's first two vessels, was the company's first vessel with a Barlow marine elevator, and was fitted with a 100-hp diesel. She generally ran the Olympia-Seattle route. The freighter is seen here on a warm summer day with all its deckhouse doors open for ventilation.

ARRIVING AT THE CANADIAN NATIONAL PIER, the *Capitol* crew prepares to tie up and unload her cargo from Olympia. As business increased, PSFL reorganized into two separate companies, Puget Sound Freight and Ferry Lines, and the Capitol Line. The freighter hulls were usually painted buff and black, with red and black stacks that later were painted buff and black. On June 15, 1937 the *Capitol* caught fire near Harstine Island and burned up so fast that Capt. Homer Stroup and the crew had barely enough time to lower a boat.

THE *WARRIOR* WAS LAUNCHED AT WESTERN BOATBUILDING in Tacoma in 1936, 418 tons, with twin Atlas Imperial diesels of 200 hp each, giving her a speed of ten knots. Built of steel, she was designed by Capt. Frank E. Lovejoy and his son Howard. She is shown here on sea trials after her launching. A year later PSFL purchased the steel *L.P. Hosford,* of 1931, from the Shaver Forwarding Co., towed it to Lake Washington Shipyard with the tug *Tyee* and rebuilt it there as the *Indian,* with a new deck and deckhouse similar to those of the *Warrior.*

A DECK VIEW OF THE *WARRIOR* in 1936, soon after her Tacoma launching, with the Seattle skyline behind.

THE *WARRIOR* AT THE CANADIAN NATIONAL DOCK in 1936 is shown here, just prior to receiving her first load of cargo for PSFL. In the late 1930s the *Warrior*, the *Indian*, and the *Seatac* carried 2,500 tons of freight daily between Seattle and Tacoma. In 1959 the *Warrior* was converted to a barge, in tow of the chartered tug *Bee*, of 1901, and later the cannery tender *Narada*, of 1919.

ON MAY 23, 1938, CAPT. FRANK E. LOVEJOY ENTERED THE *INDIAN* IN A RACE with the *Aleutian Native*, in spirit honoring such speedy steamers as the *Princess Victoria, Greyhound, Bailey Gatzert, Flyer,* and *T.J. Potter.* However, the *Indian* lost the race due to an engine breakdown. Not one to give up so easily, Lovejoy challenged the sternwheel steamer *Skagit Chief* to a Fourth of July race, and this time won soundly. He then challenged all comers to a Labor Day race, but had no takers. Capt. Lovejoy was at this time in charge of eight Puget Sound freighters which made about sixty different stops, probably the high point of his career before "crossing the bar" October 4, 1940.

THE *ALEUTIAN NATIVE,* WITH TWIN SIX-CYLINDER WASHINGTON DIESELS of 200 hp each, took the honors on Maritime Day, May 23, 1938.

THE *SKOOKUM CHIEF* CAUGHT FIRE IN 1935, burned to her main deck, and was beached on Steamboat Island near Olympia, Washington, just before sinking. Though declared a total loss, she was salvaged and rebuilt by Western Boat Co. at Tacoma and was returned to service. The *Skookum Chief* was originally built as the *K.L. Ames* at Seattle in 1915, 184 tons, as a sternwheel steam cannery tender for the Northwestern Fisheries Co. She was fitted with twin single-cylinder steam engines, 12 x 60, of 300 hp. In 1928 she was purchased by PSFL and rebuilt into a twin-screw, 200 hp diesel freighter with a cargo capacity of 300 tons. In 1959 she was converted to a barge and six years later was sold to Glacier Bay Fish Co., repowered, and used as a tender in the Alaska fisheries.

THE STEEL DIESEL FREIGHTER *F.E. LOVEJOY* WAS BUILT by Reliable Welding Works near Olympia. Designed by Carl Nordstrom, she was 178 feet overall and 613 tons. The freighter was fitted with a 10-ton Barlow marine elevator to load and unload 800 tons of cargo from two decks, with the help of gas-powered lift trucks. Powered by a six-cylinder, 16 x 20 Fairbanks-Morse direct-reversing two-cycle diesel engine producing 1,200 hp. at 300 rpm, which turned an eight-foot bronze propeller, she made eleven knots. Reliable Welding is now known as Reliable Steel Fabricators, and is at the same location (see page 207).

WELDED STEEL CONSTRUCTION was a relatively new technique, when the Lovejoy was built, having been introduced in the mid-1930s. However, Reliable Welding Works had a great deal of experience, as they had recently built twenty-two steel Army tugs during World War II.

LAUNCHED IN APRIL OF 1946, THE *F.E. LOVEJOY* was the flagship of the PSFL fleet. Generally used on the Seattle–Powell River, B.C. route, she carried newsprint for Seattle papers. The last of Puget Sound's inland freighters, she managed to make scheduled runs until July 1971, when she was laid up on Lake Union alongside the *Indian* and the *Warrior*, then was sold and converted to the Alaskan fish processor *Denali*. PSFL continued in the marine freight business until May of 1998, with their freighters replaced by the 75-foot Marco-built steel tugs *Edith Lovejoy*, and the *Anne Carlander,* and barges *Skagit, Dungeness, Swinomish,* and *Tumwater*. In June of 1999 the two tugs and barges *Tumwater, Whidbey, Cape Flattery,* and *Barkley Sound* are occasionally chartered to Sound Freight Lines, thus continuing one tradition of the Northwest inland marine freight business. PSFL is still in business, now as Puget Sound Truck Lines.

THE STERNWHEEL STEAMBOAT *SKAGIT CHIEF* was built by Lake Union Dry Dock and Machine Works. Although built in 1935, she resembled a nineteenth-century steamboat. She replaced the Skagit River Navigation and Trading Co.'s *Harvester*, which was sunk in 1934 by the *President Madison*. Using the single-cylinder steam engines of 400 hp from the *G.K. Wentworth*, of 1905, and fitted with spuds to hoist her over sandbars, she ran the Seattle–Stanwood–Mount Vernon–La Conner route.

THE *SKAGIT CHIEF* ENGAGED IN A HIGHLY SPIRITED STEAMBOAT RACE in 1938, but lost to the *Indian*. In 1950, during Seattle's Seafair celebration, she took part in a historic race between the last three active sternwheel steamers on Puget Sound. Again she lost, this time to the *Skagit Belle* and *W.T. Preston*. The *Skagit Chief* was sold to the Portland Harbor Marina and, in tow of the *Martha Foss*, foundered off Grays Harbor on October 29, 1956.

GOVERNMENT VESSELS LIKE THE STEAM STERNWHEELER *W.T. PRESTON,* played an important role in Pacific Northwest maritime history. This U.S. Army Corps of Engineers snagboat now rests on a permanent drydock next to the railway station in Anacortes. The *Preston* has a somewhat complicated history, dating back to the steamer *Swinomish* which worked on Puget Sound as a freight, passenger, and tow boat. That wooden vessel was purchased by the Army Corps of Engineers in 1914 and rebuilt at Winslow in 1915 into the first *W.T. Preston.* In 1929 she was rebuilt again. Ten years later a new steel *W.T. Preston* was constructed at Lake Union Dry Dock, using the machinery and other items from the old *W.T. Preston.* This second *Preston* worked continuously until her retirement in the 1980s.

THE STERNWHEEL STEAM TOWBOAT *PORTLAND,* owned by the Port of Portland, was the second vessel of her type to carry that name. Built in 1947, of 928 tons, to replace the first *Portland,* of 1919, most people assumed she would be a modern oil screw tug similar to what had commonly been built for the last twenty-five years. However, it was thought the steam powered, 1500 hp sternwheel design would be better suited for river work. She was run by the Shaver Transportation Co., and in 1952 raced against the old 1912 Shaver steam towboat *Henderson,* but lost. When constructed, the *Henderson,* of 430 tons, received a new locomotive boiler, although it used 1901-vintage engines, of 800 hp. The *Portland* proves that things don't change very fast in the steam towboat business. She worked until about 1981, and is now a museum ship in Portland.

IN JUNE OF 1933 THE U.S. FRIGATE *CONSTITUTION*, which had been recently restored by funds raised by school children, made a visit to Seattle's Pier 40-41 (now Pier 90-91) in tow of the minesweeper *Grebe*. This oldest surviving vessel of the U.S. Navy, known as "Old Ironsides," visited ninety U.S. ports from 1931 to 1934 and was toured by more than four million people. She was built at Boston, 2,200 gt, in 1797; between 1992 and 1996 she underwent her fourth restoration.

THE US *SC-302*, was one of twenty-five wooden subchasers of 110 feet built at the Puget Sound Naval Shipyard at Bremerton for World War I service. The shipyard turned out a variety of naval vessels during that time. She was fitted with three 200-hp Standard open base gasoline engines with ignitors, and could make seventeen knots. She carried two 30-caliber Browning belt-fed machine guns on the bridge, a Y-gun at the stern, and a "6-pounder" mounted on the foredeck. Subchasers such as these also carried three types of sound detectors mounted beneath the hull to determine the distance and direction of their target. *SC-302* was launched in 1917, for Pacific Coast duty, and was stationed first at Pichlinique, Mexico, then off the Central American coast. The ship eventually transited the Panama Canal and arrived at Florida at the war's end. She was decommissioned at the end of 1918, and was sold to Cuba.

THE "BLACK GANG," SHOWN HERE ON THE DECK OF THE US *SC-302,* were responsible for keeping the three engines running. Machinist Mate First Class John Snapp is on the left. Although the *SC-302* was the latest thing in small Naval vessels during World War I, she worked alongside nineteenth-century coal burning, square rigged ships, such as the 1,000-ton displacement third-rate barkentine *Vicksburg.* A total of 235 similar subchasers crossed the Atlantic under their own power to serve in the eastern theatre; they were credited with sinking forty per cent of all the U-boats lost in World War I.

THE USS *SAN SABA*, *APA 232* RETURNS TO *PIER* 90 at Seattle's Smith Cove in October 1945, after a year in the South Pacific. One of thirty-one victory transports built by the Kaiser Co. at Vancouver, Washington, she was of 7,650 tons, and powered by twin steam turbines that developed 9,000 hp for a maximum speed of eighteen knots. Another thirty-four similar transports were built by Oregon Shipbuilding Co. of Portland, which had just previously built 330 liberty ships. The speed of the Victory transports was a great improvement over the speed of the earlier liberty ships, which had traditional triple expansion steam engines of 2,500 hp, and made eleven knots. Of about 2,930 libertys built during World War II, only a few still exist in the late 1990s. The *San Saba* was launched on November 12, 1944, and could accommodate 1,575 troops along with 555 officers and men in ship's company. She was equipped with twenty-six landing boats; armament included one 40-mm quad, four 40-mm twins, ten 20-mm machine guns, and one 5-3/8-inch dual purpose surface-to-air gun.

THE U.S. NAVY SARGO CLASS SUBMARINE *193* (right) moored at Pier 41 in Seattle attracts a crowd.

THE U.S. COAST GUARD HARBOR CUTTER *GUARD* transits the Ballard Locks. Built in 1914 at Mare Island, California, of 52 tons, she was fitted with a triple-expansion steam engine with an oil-fired boiler, and made ten knots. She was later fitted with a diesel engine. First stationed at Friday Harbor in Washington's San Juan Islands, she was taken over by the Navy during World War II and decommissioned in 1943. The square rigged ship in the background is the *St. Paul*.

THE U.S. LIGHTHOUSE TENDER *HEATHER*, BUILT AT THE MORAN YARD IN SEATTLE in 1903, of 631 tons, was constructed of steel, and was fitted with a compound steam engine and two single-end Scotch boilers that produced 685 hp. The *Heather* was built alongside the USS *Nebraska*, the only U.S. Navy battleship to be built in the Northwest. The *Heather* maintained the aids to navigation on Puget Sound until 1940, when she was replaced by the lighthouse tender *Fir*. She was used by the U.S. Army during World War II as the *FS-534* and nearly scrapped after the war, but found her way to Hong Kong in 1948 as a coastal trader on the Chinese coast.

THE ANCHORAGE AND BOARDING CUTTER *AB-68* heads toward the Puget Sound Freight Line ships *Indian* and *Warrior*. The patrol boat, built in 1936 at Terminal Island, California, had a 150-hp diesel and made eight knots.

THE COAST GUARD PATROL BOAT *4323* comes alongside the Coast Guard cutter *Atalanta* (left). Built by the Stevens Bros. at Stockton, California, about 1936, she was powered with a Murray and Tregurtha six-cylinder gas engine of 325 hp.

THE U.S. LIGHTHOUSE TENDER *MANZANITA* lies at Ballard, in Seattle, next to the drydocked purse seiner *Washington.* One of several steel sisterships built at Camden, New Jersey in 1908, of 1,057 tons, she steamed to the west coast by way of the Straits of Magellan, accompanied by sister tenders *Sequoia* and *Kukui,* and lightships *93, 88,* and *92.* This tender is sometimes confused with the older wooden US LHT *Manzanita,* of 1879, 297 tons, which was rebuilt into the steam tug *Daniel Kern* on the Columbia River in 1905.

THE U.S. COAST GUARD CUTTER *ALGONQUIN* (right) was constructed by the Globe Iron Works at Toledo Ohio in 1898 along with a sistership, the *Onondaga.* They were built for the U.S. Revenue Cutter Service in cooperation with the U.S. Navy for use in the Spanish American War, although they did not see action. These 736-ton propeller steamers carried a complement of seven officers and forty men. In 1917 the *Algonquin* was taken over by the Navy and was stationed in the European theatre during World War I, where she remained until 1919. After being turned over to the Coast Guard, she was based in Astoria, Oregon, and was used on North Pacific and Bering Sea patrols until November 1927. She was briefly dispatched to San Francisco to chase Prohibition-era rumrunners, but returned a few months later. Retired in 1931, she was sold to Foss Launch and Tug Co. She is shown here at their Seattle yard, where she remained for a number of years. In 1940, after Puget Sound Bridge and Dredging installed a 1,200 kilowatt generator, she was towed by the *Patricia Foss* (former Revenue-Cutter *Arcata,* of 1903) to Kodiak, Alaska, where she assisted in air base construction.

THE STEAMSHIP *CANADIAN PRINCESS*, FORMERLY THE *WILLIAM J. STEWART*, is seen here as a hotel ship, an adjunct to a sports fishing lodge in Ucluelet, B.C. Built at Collingwood, Ontario, in 1932 to replace the survey ship *Lillooet* of 1908, the 228-foot *Stewart* worked the B.C. coast for the Canadian Hydrographic Service for forty-three years. Due to the ample supply of coal at Nanaimo and Union Bay, she was not converted to burn oil until 1958. In June of 1944 she had the unfortunate luck of striking Ripple Rock at Seymour Narrows, but was able to make the beach before sinking, where she remained for a month. Retired in 1975, she was converted to a hotel ship in 1979, and so remains in good condition today.

ESCORTED BY WILLITS CANOES, the three-masted bark *Eagle* arrives at Seattle on August 3, 1965. This book's author was with a group of canoeists asked to escort the Coast Guard training ship upon her arrival to Seattle for Seafair. Built in Germany in 1936 as the *Horst Wessel*, 1,816 tons displacement, with an eight-cylinder, 730-hp diesel auxiliary, she carries about 20,000 square feet of sails. She was taken by the U.S. government as a war prize at the end of World War II. Nearly every officer in the U.S. Coast Guard has served on her.

THE *MOBY DICK*, SEEN HERE IN USE BY H.W. McCURDY in September of 1939, had many uses over the years. She was built as the *Olympic* for Frank Wright of the Carlyle Packing Co. for use as an inspection boat. Wright owned the 1879 steam bark USS *Nipsic*, 1,375 tons displacement, and much of the hardware installed came from the *Nipsic*, including inch-thick glass portlights. In 1917 the *Olympic* was requisitioned for use during World War I as the patrol boat *State*. After the war she was used by the U.S. Public Health Service as the quarantine boat *Preston H. Bailhache*. Retired from government service in 1934, she was purchased by H.W. McCurdy who restored her, renamed her *Moby Dick*, and installed the bell from the five-masted 1878 schooner *Snow and Burgess*, which he had scrapped about ten years earlier. Requisitioned again by the U.S. government during World War II, the *Moby Dick* was later used as a U.S. mail boat on the Anacortes–San Juan Islands run by Earl Butler of Lopez Island. She started this service in 1962, replacing the *Bristol*, of 1928, which had recently foundered in Rosario Strait.

THE UNIVERSITY OF WASHINGTON RESEARCH VESSEL *CATALYST* heads out to Puget Sound for oceanographic research. The *Catalyst* was built at Lake Union Drydock and Machine Works in 1932 at a time of very little shipbuilding activity. Of 91 tons, she is powered by a 120 hp six-cylinder heavy duty Washington diesel, which is still running today.

THE U.S. LIGHTSHIP *SWIFTSURE No. 113*, is shown here after she has left her station at Swiftsure Bank in May of 1938, and has returned to Seattle for annual maintenance. The lightship *Relief No. 83* took her place. Though all lightships were painted red with white letters after 1940, when the Coast Guard took over responsibility of lightships, in this photo she is yellow with black letters, to differentiate her from the lightship *Umatilla Reef,* stationed just twenty-two miles south. The *Swiftsure* normally carried a complement of fifteen men for maintaining her light and fog horn, and keeping her anchored on station.

THE LIGHTSHIP *SWIFTSURE* is seen here moored at Gig Harbor, Washington, in 1972. She was one of the first diesel-electric lightships. Declared surplus in 1968, she was brought to Gig Harbor to be used as a museum ship. However, the Coast Guard reclaimed her in 1975 because she was not being properly maintained, and sold her at auction to be scrapped.

TWO VETERAN FIREBOATS, THE *DUWAMISH* AND THE *ALKI*, patrolled the Seattle waterfront for decades. The *Duwamish*, at left, built by the Richmond Beach Shipbuilding Co., joined the fire department in 1909. She was fitted with two double vertical 1,100 hp steam engines (14, 16) and four Mosher water tube boilers. When she was rebuilt at Winslow in 1949 her engines were replaced by three Cooper-Bessemer diesel-electrics. She helped put out the July 29, 1914, fire which destroyed the Grand Trunk Pacific Pier, and patrolled the waterfront until August 1984. The *Duwamish* was replaced by the *Chief Seattle*, but was preserved by the Shipping and Railway Heritage Trust and is still operable today.

The *Alki* still works today for the Seattle Fire Department. Launched in 1927 at Pacific Coast Engineering Co. in Oakland, California, with seven Winton 350-hp gasoline engines. Six of these engines powered her centrifugal fire pumps, which could throw about 17,000 gallons of water a minute. In 1947 twin GM 8-268 Cleveland diesels of 500 hp each from World War II surplus YTM minesweepers were installed, as were six twin sets of GM 6-71 diesels designed to run her six main fire pumps.

SNAPPSHOTS

Three historic fishing schooners are still floating today. 1) The Bendixsen-built lumber, and later cod fishing, schooner Wawona of 1897, is shown here under Robinson Fisheries ownership in 1937. 2) The Wawona, now part of Northwest Seaport's historic fleet, being restored on Lake Union. 3) The Nova Scotia built ex-Grand Banker Robertson II of 1940, now a sail training schooner based in Victoria, in drydock at Point Hope Shipyard, Victoria, (see pages 30-31). 4) The Bendixsen-built lumber and codfishing schooner C.A.Thayer of 1895.

Note: All photos in this section are described clockwise from upper left, or from top to bottom.

1) The Hansville, Washington steamer dock undergoing repairs in 1938. 2) The steamer *Hyak*, arriving at a Seattle pier about 1933. 3) The gas passenger launch *Falcon* at Everett, 1920.

The Washington Navigation Co. ran ferries from Tacoma's Point Defiance to Gig Harbor until 1950. 1) The dock was located just inside the entrance to the harbor. 2) The ferry Vashonia, rebuilt from the gas ferry Relief in 1932, lies at her slip in the harbor; she was dismantled in 1951. 3) The Skansonia, was one of the ferries that ran from Point Defiance.

1) The Kirkland ferry dock, in 1915. Lots at Kirkland were advertised for $75.00 at that time. 2) The ferry *Mount Vernon* operated on the Anacortes-Sidney, B.C., and Port Townsend-Keystone routes in the 1920s. 3) The steam ferry *San Mateo* retires to Eagle Harbor on Labor Day, 1969, (see page 141). 4) The *Quillayute* ran the Port Ludlow–Edmonds route.

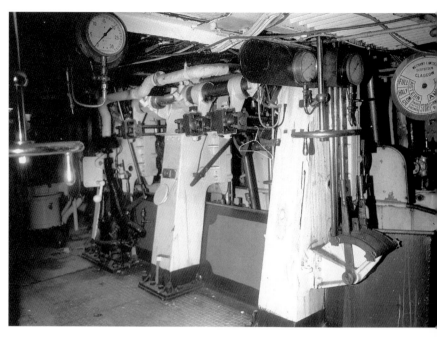

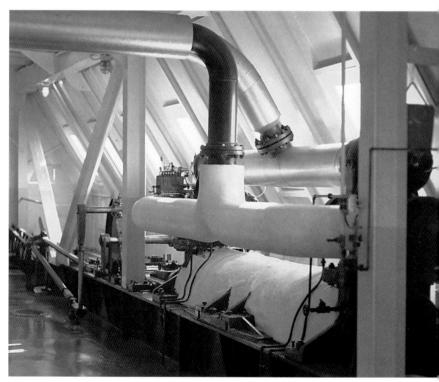

1) Keith Sternberg works on the cross-head guides prior to the installation of the reground crankshaft on the triple-expansion steam engine of the *Virginia V*. 2) One of the two triple-expansion steam engines of the *Canadian Princess* (ex-*William J. Stewart*). Note the telegraph, gauges and controls.

3) Port engine of the steamer *Portland* producing 800 hp. Just visible is the 36-foot Pittman arm connecting to the 25-foot diameter by 26-foot wide sternwheel. 4) The fireroom of the *San Mateo*, showing the three water tube oil fired boilers (see page 149).

1) A sad ending for the steam sternwheeler *Skagit Belle*. She sank next to Seattle's Coleman Dock in 1965. Built in Seattle in 1941, her steam engines came from the steamer *Umatilla* of 1908. 2) The Ramano diving bell, with help from the tug *Trio* made an unsucessful attempt to salvage the tug *Bahada* off Saddlebag Island near Anacortes, Washington in the mid 1930s. 3) A waterline view of the *Pacific Spruce* and *Pacific Redwood* shows the riveted steel of in-and-out plating construction. 4) The *Foss 300* steam crane built for World War II service is still in active use in the late 1990s.

1) The tug *Calumet*, working for Samson Tug and Barge, travels light near Sitka, Alaska. 2) A Campbell Towing ex-YTM tug returns to Wrangell, Alaska. 3) The tug *Elf* at anchor near Friday Harbor, Washington. 4) The tug *Gillking*, shown working for the Gilley Bros. along the British Columbia coast, tows logs for Pacific Towing today.

1) The *Marlin II*, shown moored at Tacoma, was built in 1906 as the steam tug *Clayburn*. 2) The *Drew Foss*, built by Foss at their Tacoma yard, tows a log boom near Whidbey Island. In the late 1990s her homeport is Victoria, B.C. 3)

The oldest running tug in the Northwest, the *Rustler*, 20 tons, was built at Hoquiam in 1887, and in 1999 is moored at Poulsbo. 4) The *Arthur Foss*, the *F.L. Fulton*, and the steam lightship *Swiftsure* at Ballard.

1) The tug *Favorite*, built for Tacoma Tug and Barge Co. in 1937, 8 tons, with a 130-hp Hall Scott diesel, lays at Kingston. 2) The tug *Skagit Chief* waits for the Dunlap chip barge to finish loading at Olympia. 3) The big steam tug *Tyee* was built by Hiram Doncaster and William A. McCurdy at Port Ludlow, 317 tons, in 1884, for the Pope and Talbot Co. was finishing a tow job for Merrill & Ring Lumber Co. at Pysht, Washington, in 1935.

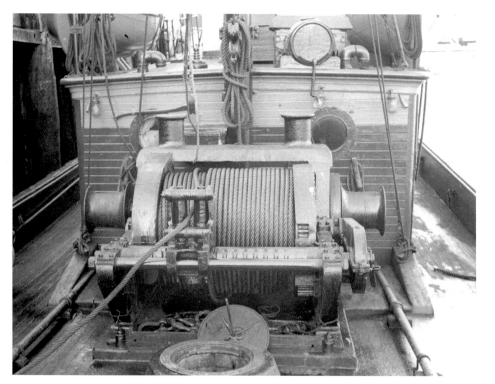

1) The towing winch, the business end of the Grays Harbor tug *Tyee.* 2) The former ST Army tug, *Sigrid H,* of Manke Lumber Co., waits for a towing job near Shelton, Washington. 3) LT Army tugs for sale in Seattle, three at a time.

4) Engineer of the cannery tender *David B* checks the timing of the 1929 three-cylinder Washington-Estep diesel, 100 hp at 300 rpm.

1) The tug *Quail*, built in Alaska for fishing tender work in Bristol Bay, and now based at Anacortes, assists in the rebuilding of the marina at Friday Harbor, Washington. 2) The steel tug *North Bend* performs ship assist work in Coos Bay, Oregon. 3)The tug *Trio*, of 1911, was built by the Reid Bros., Decatur Island, Washington, as a steam shrimper. She was later used as a tug by Cary-Davis Towing Co., Shively Tug Boat Co., and Pioneer Towing Co. 4) Puget Sound Freight Lines Terminal, and the barge *Whidbey* and tug *Anne Carlander* on the West Waterway, Seattle.

1) Miki Tug *Dominion* at Point Hope Shipyard, Victoria, B.C.
2) The little tug *Koos No.2* of 1924, is now a museum boat at
Coos Bay, Oregon. 3. The passenger launch *Hyack*, ex-
Ticaboo, ex-*Hyack*, built at Dockton, Washington in 1906, was
later used as a log patrol boat, and is under restoration on
Lopez Island in the 1990's. 4) The tug *Chickamauga* of 1915,
with her four-cylinder Nelseco engine, was the first diesel
powered tug in the U.S.

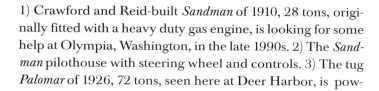

1) Crawford and Reid-built *Sandman* of 1910, 28 tons, originally fitted with a heavy duty gas engine, is looking for some help at Olympia, Washington, in the late 1990s. 2) The *Sandman* pilothouse with steering wheel and controls. 3) The tug *Palomar* of 1926, 72 tons, seen here at Deer Harbor, is powered by an Atlas Imperial diesel of 320 hp at 325 rpm. 4) The Prothero-built tug *Susan H,* of 1947, 39 tons, nudges a gravel barge onto the beach at Lopez Island, 1985. 5) Ex-Foss tug *Joe,* 15 tons, of 1942, is still in excellent working order in 1999.

1) Ex-Army freighter, *T-482*, the Sea Explorer ship *Whidby,* delivers Santa and his toys to children on the San Juan Islands. 2) The Alaska Packers Association launch *Plover* of 1944, 12 tons, was restored by volunteers in the 1990s at Blaine, Washington. 3) The *Pintail* and *Nordland* race towards Anacortes from the San Juan Islands. 4) The last bargeload of San Juan Island sand and gravel, in tow of the tug *Tom White,* is delivered to Lopez Island, on March 6, 1999.

1) The Canadian park-type liberty ship, *Cape Breton*, at North Vancouver in 1999, was to be scuttled, as there was not enough interest in preserving this historic steamer. 2) The Phillip Spaulding designed, Black Ball Transportation Co. *Coho* of 1959, 5,360 tons, like her predecessor the *Chinook* of 1947, 5,500 tons, influenced B.C. and Alaska coastal ferries for many years. 3) The steamship *W.M. Tupper,* built by the Merrill-Stevens Co. in 1917, 1,852 tons, was a well known Arctic trader owned by the Santa Ana Steamship Co. from 1924 to 1938.

1) and 2) The varnished wheelhouse and twin stacks of the steamship *Princess Marguerite* as they appeared on her last run from Victoria to Seattle in September, 1989. These features were typical of steamships built on the Clyde River in Scotland during the 1940s and earlier. 3) CNR's last steamer, *Prince George*, shown here in layup at the Britannia Mines in 1994, was built by Yarrows Ltd. at Esquimalt, B.C. in 1948, of 5,812 tons. She ran on the Alaska cruise route. A fire ended her career in 1975, though she was later converted to a hotel ship and used at Expo 86. Following two fires in October, 1995, she was sold to be scrapped in October 1996. On her way to the Far East, in tandem with the tanker *Vicky Ray* (ex-USS *Kishwaugee AOG-09*), in tow of the tug *Pacific Challenger*, the vessels encountered a severe storm.

The *Prince George* foundered near Dutch Harbor, Alaska, but the tug and tanker survived. The tanker, along with another ship in tandem tow of the *Pacific Challenger* continued toward the Far East; however, when besieged by another storm off the Japanese coast, the tug made it to port, both ships in tow foundered.

1) The view from the Ballard Locks looking east about 1934. Note the first *W.T. Preston*, rebuilt from the steamer *Swinomish* of 1903, 166 tons, and yards of the ship *St. Paul*, at left. 2) The Japanese ship *Hie Maru*, loading scrap iron for Japan was not a popular ship in 1940. Note the Puget Sound Freight Lines *Seatac* at right. 3) The *President Madison* shown here in serious trouble when she rolled over and was partially submerged on March 23, 1933, while steel plating was being repaired on her starboard bow at Todd Dry Docks, Inc.

1) The view from the Ballard Locks looking Southeast about 1938. Note the Estep Engine Co., the US LHT *Manzanita* (see page 178), the U.S. Lighthouse Depot, and the Lightship *Relief*. 2) The *Pacific Redwood* and the *Pacific Spruce* in layup on Lake Union in the 1930's. Due to the Depression these vessels, though only about twelve years old, sold for $10,000 to $15,000 in 1932. 3) Todd Pacific Shipyard at Harbor Island in the 1990s.

1) Reliable Steel Fabricators, formerly Reliable Welding Works (see pages 161–162) continues building steel vessels, however the new vessels are designed to contain liquids. 2) Note the crane, which was used in the construction of the *F.E. Lovejoy* in 1946. 3) George Broom started sewing square sails in 1910 on Pier 8, and his son Rupert worked in the family business until his death in 1994, sailing to work every day from Port Madison. George's grandson, George Broom, took over operations which now generally consist of rigging, canvas work, and steady sails. The company has been at this location since 1972. 4) Lake Union Drydock, in business since 1919, repairs not only steel, but wooden ships. They rebuilt the steamer *Virginia V,* of 1922, in the late 1990s.

Left: 1) Vessels in lay-up near the Ballard Oil dock include (from left) a steel fishing vessel, the tuna/sardine clipper *Ronnie S*, ex-*YP-627*, of 1945, the motorship *Helena Star*, just visible tug *Florence Fillberg*, and retired Army and Navy tugs including the *Vigorous* and *Sea Fox*, at right. 2)The *Catalyst* receives preventive maintenance every spring. Here Stephen Snapp replaces a small section of boat deck coaming. 3) Northwest Seaport's *Arthur Foss* of 1889, has her forward bulwarks and caps replaced in 1999, courtesy of Bates boatbuilding students at Tacoma. She is in better condition now than she has been in years, partly because she is not a static display, but is used every year (see page 40).

1) The remains of the steam schooner *Sierra*, in the late 1990s, lie not far from where she was built at Hoquiam, Washington in 1916 (see page 81). 2) Robert Moran's estate and his yacht *San Wan* on Orcas Island, in Washington's San Juan Islands, about 1916. Moran began his career in the Pacific Northwest in 1875 as a logging camp cook.

1) With cargo booms on deck, the steam schooner *A.G. Lindsay*, on Elliott Bay about 1915, prepares to steam north to Alaska (see page 76). 2) Roche Harbor Lime Co. on northwest San Juan Island, loading lime barrels onto a three-masted schooner about 1916.

1) Eagledale, Washington, still has a working waterfront. Note the various tugs and barges moored here including, from left, the little scow schooner, tug hull *Crowley 23*, various barges, the ex-YTL tug *James B*, a tuna troller, the tug *Elmore* of 1890 (see page 60) next to the retired Washington State Ferry *Olympic* of 1938, and the halibut schooner *Thor* of 1925.
2) The Snohomish River near Everett, Washington, is another working waterfront. Note the Miki tug *Dominion* , built at Hoquiam in 1944, 290 tons, still in excellent working order, and large fishing vessels such as the *Deep Sea,* at right.

BIBLIOGRAPHY

Andrews, Ralph W. and Harry A. Kirwin. *This Was Seafaring.* Seattle: Superior Publishing Co., 1955.

Andrews, Ralph W. and A. K. Larssen. *Fish and Ships.* Seattle: Superior Publishing Co., 1959.

Benson, Richard M. *Steamships and Motorships of the West Coast.* Seattle: Superior Publishing Co., 1968.

Carey, Roland. *The Sound of Steamers.* Seattle: Alderbrook Publishing Co., 1965.

DeLong, Harriet Tracy. *Pacific Schooner "Wawona."* Bellevue, Washington: Documentary Book Publishers Corp., 1985.

Farber, Jim. *Steamer's Wake.* Seattle: Enetai Press, 1985.

Hitchman, James H. *A Maritime History of the Pacific Coast of America 1540–1980.* University Press of America. 1990.

Kline, M. S. *Steamboat Virginia V.* Bellevue, Washington: Documentary Book Publishers Corporation, 1985.

Merchant Vessels of the United States. Washington, D.C.: U.S. Government Printing Office, printed annually.

Morgan, Murray. *Puget's Sound: A Narrative of Early Tacoma and the Southern Sound.* Seattle: University of Washington Press, 1979.

——. and Rosa Morgan. *South on the Sound.* Woodland Hills, Washington: Windsor Publications, Inc., 1984.

Morris, Rob. *Coasters.* Canada: Horsdal and Schubart Publishers, Ltd., 1993.

Musk, George. *Canadian Pacific Afloat, 1883–1968.* Warrington, England: Canadian Pacific. 1968.

Newell, Gordon, ed. *The H.W. McCurdy Marine History of the Pacific Northwest, 1895–1965.* Seattle: Superior Publishing Co., 1966.

——. *The H.W. McCurdy Marine History of the Pacific Northwest, 1966–1975.* Seattle: Superior Publishing Co., 1977.

——. *Pacific Steamboats.* Seattle: Superior Publishing Co., 1958.

——. *Ships of the Inland Sea.* Portland: Binfords and Mort, 1951.

——. and Joe Williamson. *Pacific Coastal Liners.* Seattle: Superior Publishing Co., 1959.

——. *Pacific Lumber Ships.* Seattle: Superior Publishing Company, 1960.

——. *Pacific Tugboats.* Seattle: Superior Publishing Company, 1957.

Pacific Motor Boat. Vol. 37, No. 12, November 1945.

Passport to Ballard. Seattle: Ballard News Tribune, 1988.

Puget Sound Bridge and Dredging–A Record of Achievement, 1886–1946. Seattle: Puget Sound Bridge and Dredging, 1947.

The Sea Chest, Journal of the Puget Sound Maritime Historical Society. Seattle. Published quarterly 1967-present. Various issues.

Skalley, Mike. *100 Years of Foss History.* Seattle, 1990.

Timmen, Fritz. *Blow for the Landing.* Caldwell: The Caxton Printers, Ltd., 1973.

Williamson, Joe and Jim Gibbs. *Maritime Memories of Puget Sound.* Seattle: Superior Publishing Co., 1976.

Wright, E.W., ed. *Lewis and Dryden Marine History of the Pacific Northwest.* Portland, Oregon: Lewis and Dryden Publishing Company, 1896.

APPENDIX

A NOTE ABOUT TONNAGE

Measurements of vessels in this book, unless otherwise noted, are registered, or interior volume measurements in tons, with one ton equal to 100 cubic feet.

Gross tonnage (gt) is the entire volume, or total enclosed spaces, of a ship, including deckhouses.

Net tonnage (nt) is the gross tonnage, less non-revenue-earning space, i.e. less tankage, crew's quarters, machinery spaces, bunkers, etc.

Deadweight tonnage is the actual total weight, measured in long tons of 2240 lbs, that a vessel can carry and still remain seaworthy.

Displacement tonnage is the actual weight of water a ship displaces, also measured in long tons. Unless otherwise noted, such as for U.S. naval ships, it is not used here. Unless noted, the tonnage figures mentioned in the text are gross tons.

MEASUREMENTS

Vessel length measurements in the text are generally the length on deck, not including spars, unless otherwise noted. Registered vessel measurements given in the appendix are listed as follows: length x breadth x depth, depth refering to depth of hold and not draft. The register dimensions of U.S. flagged vessels are in feet and tenths of feet, and are officially described as follows (1936): The length from the fore part of the outer planking on the side of the stem to the after part of the main stern post of screw steamers, and to the after part of the rudder post of all other vessels measured on the top of the tonnage deck, shall be accounted the vessel's length. The breadth of the broadest part on the outside of the vessel shall be accounted the vessel's breadth of beam. A measure from the underside of the tonnage deck plank, amidships, to the ceiling of the hold (average thickness), shall be accounted the depth of hold. (Rev. Stat., sec 4150)

PHOTOGRAPHIC DETAILS AND DATES

The photographs in this book are listed below with additional vessel details, followed by the date of the photo. All photos by John Farrington Snapp are labeled J.F.S. All photos by Jeremy Sherman Snapp are labeled J.S.S.

PAGE

11 Four-masted bark *Thielbeck*, ex-*Prince Robert*, later *David Dollar*, steel, 1893, Liverpool, Great Britain. 2831 gt. August 22, 1913–J.F.S.

12 Three-masted bark *Marco Polo*, steel, 1892, Great Britain. 1620 gt
   Sternwheel steamer *Ocklhama*, 1875, rebuilt 1897, Portland, Or. 676 gt, 565 nt, 161.1 x 33.5 x 8.3. July 19, 1913–J.F.S.

13 Downeaster ship *Elwell*, 1875, Damarscotta, Me. 1461 gt, 1356 nt, 212.3 x 39.1 x 24.7. April 16, 1916–J.F.S.

14–15 *Elwell , as previously described.* April 16, 1916–J.F.S.

PAGE

16 *Elwell , as previously described.*
   Steam cannery tender *Philip F. Kelly*, 1901, Tacoma, Wa. 151 gt, 72 nt, 89.3 x 22.3 x 10.5. April 16, 1916–J.F.S.

17 Auxiliary three-masted schooner *Ruby*, 1902, Alameda, Ca. 345 gt, 273 nt, 132.0 x 34.0 x 9.0. May 4, 1932–J.F.S.

18 Five-masted barkentine *Forest Pride*, 1919, Aberdeen, Wa. 1600 gt, 1424 nt, 241.5 x 44.0 x 19.2. 1934–J.F.S.

19 Four-masted schooner *Sophie Christenson*, 1901, Port Blakely, Wa. 687 gt, 680 nt, (675 as built), 180.6 x 38.9 x 13.4

Three-masted schooner *Charles R. Wilson*, 1891, Fairhaven, Ca. 345 gt, 328 nt, 150.0 x 35.0 x 11.0

Three-masted schooner, *C.A. Thayer*, 1895, Bendixsen, Fairhaven, Ca. 452 gt, 390 nt, 156.0 x 36.0 x 11.8

Forest Pride, as previously described.

Five-masted schooner, *K. V. Kruse*,1920, North Bend, Or. 1728 gt, 1554 nt, 242.3 x 46.2 x 20.0

Four-masted auxiliary schooner, *La Merced*, 1917, Benicia, Ca. 2146 gt, 1938 nt, 232.0 x 42.6 x 26.6. 1937–J.F.S.

20 Four-masted schooner *C.S. Holmes*, 1893, Port Blakely, Wa. 623 gt, 556 nt, (409 as built) 162.8 x 37.0 x 11.5. 1934–J.F.S.

21 *C. S. Holmes, as previously described.* January 22, 1938–J.F.S.

22 Schooner *Commodore*, 1919, Seattle, Wa. 1526 gt, 1339 nt, 232.9 x 45.0 x 18.8. October, 1941–J.F.S.

23 Six-masted schooner *Fort Laramie*, 1919, North Bend, Or. 2240 gt, 2140 nt, 206.5 x 46 x 24.1.

Five-masted barkentine *Monitor*, 1920, Oakland, Ca. 2247 gt, 2102 nt, 264.4 x 46.0 x 24.0.

Five-masted schooner *Thistle*, 1918, St. Helens, Or. 1586 gt, 1462 nt, 240.0 x 44.0 x 20.8. 1933–J.F.S.

24 Four-masted schooner *Alumna*, 1901, North Bend, Or. 696 gt, 644 nt, 189.1 x 40.0 x 15.6. 1934-J.F.S.

25 Auxiliary schooner *Zodiac*, ex-*California*, 1924, East Boothbay, Me. 145 gt, 89 nt, 111.4 x 25.2 x 11.5. June, 1999-J.S.S.

26 Auxiliary schooner*Adventuress*, 1913, East Boothbay, Me. 78 gt, 42 nt, 85.5 x 21.4 x 9.8. September, 1979–J.S.S.

27 Auxiliary schooner *Alcyone*, 1956, Seattle, Wa. 29 gt, 27 nt, 57.1 x 15.2 x 7. September 1994–J.S.S.

28 Auxiliary bark *Endeavor* replica, 1994, Fremantle, Australia. 397 gt, 109.3 ft overall x 29.2 x 11.4. July 1999–J.S.S.

29 Auxiliary brig *Lady Washington* replica, 1989 Aberdeen,Wa. 175 tons displacement 99 gt, 53 nt, 68 ft overall x 22 x 11 draft. June 1999–J.S.S.

30–31 Auxiliary schooner *Robertson II*, 1940, Novia Scotia, 170 tons displacement, 105 ft overall x 22 ft-1 in x 11 ft-1 in draft; 5200 sq ft. sail area

Auxiliary schooner *Pacific Swift*, 1986, Vancouver, B.C. 98 tons displacement 83 ft overall x 20 ft-6 in x 10 ft-8 in draft; 2968 sq ft sail area. Febuary, 1999–J.S.S.

32 Auxiliary schooner *Pacific Grace*, under construction, launch planned October, 1999. 170 tons displacement 107 ft-10 in overall x 22 ft-2 in x 11 ft draft, 5673 sq ft. sail area. Febuary, 1999–J.S.S.

33 *Pacific Grace, as previously described.* Febuary, 1999–J.S.S.

34 Auxiliary three-masted barkentine *Regina Maris*, ex three-masted schooner *Regina*,1908, Svendborg, Denmark. 144 ft overall x 25 ft x 10 ft draft; approx. 10,000 sq ft in 42 sails. September, 1979–J.S.S.

35 Auxiliary schooner *Wander Bird*, (ex-*Wandervogel, Elbe #5)* 1883, Wevelsfleth, Germany 71 gt, 49 nt, 79.6 x 18.7 x 9.5. Febuary, 1999–J.S.S.

36 M.V. *Catalyst*, 1932, Seattle, Wa. 91 gt, 62 nt, 68.2 x 18.3 x 10.5. March, 1999–J.S.S.

37 M.V. *Westward*, 1924, Dockton, Wa. 96 gt, 65 nt, 80.2 x 18.7 x 9.4. March, 1999–J.S.S.

38 *Westward, as previously described.* March, 1999–J.S.S.

39 Foss Launch and Tug Co. Seattle moorings. 1938–J.F.S.

40 Motor tug *Arthur Foss*, ex *Wallowa*, 1889, Portland, Or. 214 gt, 118 nt, 111.6 x 23.9 x 11.6. 1933–J.F.S.

41 Motor tug *Drew Foss*, 1929, Tacoma, Wa. 34 gt, 23 nt, 53.2 x 16.0 x 7.1. July 31, 1938–J.F.S.

42 Motor tug *Lorna Foss*, ex-*Pilot*, 1903, Hoquiam, Wa. 31 gt, 21 nt, 63.1 x 13.2 x 5.8. 1933–J.F.S.

43 Yard tug on Squak Slough, possibly *Naches*   July 9, 1916–J.F.S.

44 Motor tug *Fish*, 1903, Empire City, Or. 11 gt, 9 nt, 39.7 x 11.0 x 4.2. April 21, 1939–J.F.S.

45 Steam tug *Humaconna*, steel, 1919, Superior, Wis. 418 gt, 190 nt, 142.0 x 27.5 x 14.6. June 15, 1938–J.F.S

46–47 Steam tug *Roosevelt*, 1905, Verona, Me. 618 gt, 350 nt, 182.0 x 35.5 x 16.2. 1934–J.F.S.

48 Steam tug *Wanderer*, 1890, Port Blakely, Wa. 212 gt, 125 nt, 128.2 x 23.8 x 11.4. 1933–J.F.S.

49 *Wanderer, as previously described.* 1933–J.F.S.

50 *Wanderer, as previously described.* 1933–J.F.S.

51 Motor tug *Tyee*, 1925, Hoquiam Wa. 90 gt, 61 nt, 77.1 x 20.6 x 7.6. 1937– J.F.S.

52 Motor tug *Melville*, 1903, Knappton, Wa. 70 gt, 39 nt, 85.9 x 19.7 x 7.5. March, 1936– J.F.S.

53 Steam tug *Snohomish*, steel, ex-USCG *Snohomish*, 1908 Wilmington, Del. 528 gt, 262 nt, 145.1 x 29.3 x 15.1. 1937– J.F.S.

54 Motor tug *Macray*, ex-*Mary Ellen*, 1922, Tacoma, Wa. 86 gt, 49 nt, 81.2 x 18.6 x 8.6. 1933–J.F.S.

55 Steam tug *Master*, 1922 Vancouver, B.C. 93 gt, 85 x 19 x 12 overall triple-expansion steam engine of 1918, 9.5, 15.5, 26 x 18, two-furnace Scotch fire tube boiler, 175 P.S.I. July 2, 1999-J.S.S.

56 Motor tug *Madrona*, 1923, Tacoma, Wa. 28 gt, 17 nt, 54.4 x 13.6 x 6.6. Febuary, 1999–J.S.S.

57 Motor tug *Creosote*, 1921, Seattle, Wa. 31 gt, 21 nt, 49.9 x 13.0 x 8.2. March, 1999–J.S.S.

58 Motor tug *Samson*, 1943, Seattle 92 gt, 63 nt, 76.9 x 20.0 x 10.5. August, 1979–J.S.S.

59 Motor tug *Jerrie*, 1944, Stockton, Ca. 71 gt, 28 nt, 67.4 x 17.5 x 19.1. June, 1978–J.S.S.

60 Motor tug *Kiket*, ex-*R.P. Elmore*, presently *Elmore*, 1890, Everett, Wa. 87 gt, 59 nt, 69.6 x 18.5 x 8.6. April 6,1971–J.F.S.

61 Motor tug *Dolly C*, 1922 Dockton, Wa. 56 gt, 32 nt, 66.4 x 18.6 x 7.4
　　Steamship *David W. Branch*, ex *Ecuador*, steel, 1915, Flushing, Holland. 5544 gt, 3435 nt, 380.6 x 48.7 x 24.7 triple-expansion steam engine 20, 47, 77 x 48. September, 1939–J.F.S.

62–63 Victoria's inner harbor. 1912–J.F.S.

64 C.P.R. steamship piers. 1912–J.F.S.

65 Steamship *Princess Royal*, 1907, Esquimalt, B.C. 1997 gt, 228 x 40 x 16, triple expansion steam engine
　　Steamship *Princess Adelaide*, steel, 1910, Glasgow, Scotland. 3061 gt, 290 x 46 x 17, triple-expansion steam engine. 1912–J.F.S.

66 Steamship *Princess May*, ex-*Cass*, *Arthur*, *Ningchow*, *Hating*, steel, 1888, Newcastle, England. 1394 gt, 250 x 34 x 18, triple-expansion steam engines, twin screw. 1912–J.F.S.

67 Steamship *Iroquois*, steel, 1901, Toledo, Oh. 1767 gt, 1202 nt, 213.8 x 46.0 x 15.2. August 21, 1934–J.F.S.

68 Steamship *Princess Elaine*, steel, 1927 Clydebank, Scotland. 2125 gt, 299 x 14 x 16, steam turbine, triple screw. September 1969 – J.S.S.

69 Steamship *Princess Marguerite* (2), steel, 1948, Govan, Scotland. 5911 gt, 359.5 x 56.1 x 25.8 turbo-electric, 20,500 hp. twin screw, engine room crew-36. September 19, 1989–J.S.S.

70 *Princess Marguerite* , as previously described. September 19, 1989–J.S.S.

71 Steamship *Princess Patricia* (2), steel, 1948, Govan, Scotland. 5911 gt, later 6062 gt, 359 x 56 x 25 turbo-electric, twin screw. August, 1978–J.S.S.

72 Steamship *Breakwater*, iron, 1880 Chester, Penn. 1065 gt, 793 nt, 201.0 x 30.0 x 19.3. July 21, 1913–J.F.S.

73 *Breakwater, as previously described*. August 3, 1913–J.F.S.

74–75 Seattle waterfront. June 21, 1913–J.F.S.

76 Steam schooner *A.G. Lindsay*, 1889. Detroit, Mi. 1354 gt, 1111 nt, 198.4 x 37.6 x 21.8. C. 1915–J.F.S.

77 *M.V. Wilmarth*
　　Steamer *Waialeale*, 1884, Port Blakely, Wa. 268 gt, 255 nt, 120.0 x 27.1 x 9.8 two-cylinder compound steam engine 12,22 x 18, 17 nominal hp, by Hinkley, Spiers & Hayes of San Francisco, California. C. 1915–J.F.S.

78 Steamer *Akutan*, 1913, North Bend, Or. 221 gt, 150 nt, 100.6 x 23.5 x 9.2. 1934–J.F.S.

80 Steamship *Redwood*, 1917, Bellingham Wa. 1793 gt, 1045 nt, 226.4 x 41.8 x 23.1 triple-expansion steam engine 13, 21, 35 x 24. Febuary, 1940–J.F.S.

81 Steam schooner *Cornelia*, 1917, Oakland, C. 1430 gt,. 809 nt, 223.0 x 43.6 x 16.5
　　Motor schooner *Sierra*, 1916, Hoquiam, Wa. 1510 gt,. 1199 nt, 210.6 x 42.5 x 14.8
　　Motor schooner *Dorothea*, 1910, Seattle, Wa. 116 gt,. 65 nt, 94.0 x 19.5 x 9.6. June 15, 1938–J.F.S.

82 Motorship *ZR3*, ex-*Muriel*, 1920, Houghton, Wa. 2375 gt, 1837 nt, 254.8 x 46.7 x 23.9
　　Steamship *Redwood, as previously described*
　　Steamship *International*, steel, 1919, Ashtabula, Oh. 2740 gt, 1760 nt, 253.4 x 43.7 x 26.2. 1937–J.F.S.

83 *David W. Branch, as previously described*. August, 1939–J.F.S.

84 Steamship *Yukon*, steel, ex-*Havana,* 1899, Philadelphia, Pa. 5863 gt, 3638 nt, 360.0 x 50.0 x 19.9. March, 1936–J.F.S.

85 Steamship *Alaska*, steel, 1923, Tacoma, Wa. 4658 gt, 2775 nt, 350.4 x 49.6 x 15.6. 1938–J.F.S.

86 Steamship *Admiral Farragut*, steel, 1898, Philadelphia Pa. 2141 gt, 280 ft overall. June 21, 1913-J.F.S.

87 Steamship *H.F. Alexander*, ex-*Great Northern*, ex-*Columbia*, later *General George S. Simmonds*, steel, 1914, Philadelphia Pa. 8357 gt, 3708 nt, 500.1 x 63.1 x 20.6. July, 1935–J.F.S.

88 Steamship *Haida*, steel, 1909, Sunderland, Great Britain. 3800 gt. October 22, 1937–J.F.S.

89 Steamship *Pacific Spruce*, steel, ex-*West Canon*, 1920, South San Francisco, Ca. 5509 gt, 3426 nt, 410.5 x 54.0 x 27.1
Steamship *Pacific Redwood*, steel, 1918, Seattle, Wa. 5683 gt, 3557 nt, 409.5 x 54.2 x 27.4. 1937–J.F.S.

90 Steamship *Santa Paula* steel, 1932., Kearny, N.J. 9135 gt, 3839 nt, 484.4 x 72.2 x 25.8. August 21, 1934–J.F.S.

91 Steamship *President McKinley*, steel, 1921, Camden, N.J. 14,127 gt, 8400 nt, 516.5 x 72.2 x 27.8. May 1936–J.F.S.

92 Steamship *North King*, ex-*Liebenfels*, steel, 1903, Vegesack, Germany. 5064 gt, 3386 nt, 375.7 x 50.7 x 27.3. May 1932–J.F.S.

93 Steamship *North Sea*, ex-*Plainfield, Mary Weems, Admiral Peoples*, steel, 1918, Elizabeth, N.J. 3133 gt, 1903 nt, 299.4 x 45.0 x 22.8. 1938–J.F.S.

94 Steamship *Hardanger*, steel, 1924, Port Glasgow, Scotland. 4000 gt, 2485 nt, 375.3 x 52.3 x 23.9 triple-expansion steam engine 26, 42, 70 x 48, 339 nom. hp. August 20, 1938–J.F.S.

95 *Hardanger, as previously described.* August 20, 1938–J.F.S.

96 Motor tanker *Aleutian Native*, ex-*David Campbell, Chief,* later tug *Express*, steel, 1913, Portland, Or. 240 gt, 163 nt, 118.0 x 25.1 x 10.9, twin-screw pair Washington Estep six-cylinder diesels 10.5 x 13, 200 hp at 300 rpm. May 23, 1938–J.F.S.

97 *Aleutian Native, as previously described.* 1935–J.F.S.

98 Motorship *Francis Barkley*, steel, ex-*Rennesoy*, ex-*Hidle*, 1958, Stavanger, Norway. 297 gt, 128 overall x 24 x 10. July,1999–J.S.S.

99 Motorship *Lady Rose,* steel, ex-*Lady Sylvia*, 1937, Glasgow, Scotland. 199 gt, 105 overall x 21 x 14. July,1999–J.S.S.

100 Motortanker *General*, steel, 1925, San Francisco, Ca. 570 gt, 364 nt, 170.0 x 32.0 x 14. 1937–J.F.S.

101 Lake Union Drydock and Machine Works. June 15, 1938–J.F.S.

102 Motorship *Donna Lane*, 1920, Houghton, Wa. 2185 gt, 1597 nt, 245.5 x 46.7 x 23.6. 1934–J.F.S.

103 *Donna Lane, as previously described.* 1934–J.F.S.

104 Machinist. May 18, 1938–J.F.S.

105 Steam tug *Humaconna* at L.U.D., *as previously described.* June 15, 1938–J.F.S.

106 Lake Washington Shipyard. June, 1934–J.F.S.

107 Steamship *W.M. Tupper*, steel, 1917, Jacksonville, Fl. 1756 gt, 1092 nt, 217.6 x 38.0 x 23.6
Motor schooner unidentified. June, 1934–J.F.S.

108 Shipwright (possibly Jim Warren) with H.E. Jamison February 22, 1939–J.F.S

109 Jim Warren's Marine Ways. February 22, 1939–J.F.S.

110 Bellingham Marine Railway. June, 1941–J.F.S.

111 Bellingham Marine Railway joiner shop. June, 1941–J.F.S.

112 Puget Sound Bridge and Dredging. 1938–J.F.S.

113 P.S.B.&D. 1933–J.F.S.

114 P.S.B.&D. dipper dredge. 1933–J.F.S.

115 P.S.B.&D. scow. 1938–J.F.S

116 Hart Construction pile driver. July, 1968–J.S.S.

117 Hart Construction pile driver. July, 1968–J.S.S.

118 Lake Washington Ship Canal. Ca. 1913–J.F.S.

119 Lake Washington Ship Canal dam (top). January 15, 1914–J.F.S.
Lake Washington Ship Canal (bottom). January 15, 1914–J.F.S.

120 Houseboat. October 21, 1934–J.F.S.

121 Boathouse. October 21, 1934–J.F.S.

122–123 Steamer *Virgina V*, 1922 Maplewood (Olalla), Wa. 122 gt, 83 nt, 115.9 x 24.1 x 7.1. triple-expansion steam engine 10, 17, 27 x 18, 200 rpm, 175 psi, built 1898 Heffernan Engine Works. October, 1934–J.F.S.

124 *Virgina V, as previously described.* October, 1934–J.F.S.

125 *Virginia V, as previously described.* October, 1934–J.F.S.

126 *Virginia V, as previously described.* October, 1934–J.F.S.

127 *Virginia V, as previously described.* October, 1934–J.F.S.

128 *Virginia V* before rebuild. 1933–J.F.S.

129 *Virginia V* after rebuild. July, 1935–J.F.S.

130 Steamer *Monticello*, 1906, Tacoma, Wa. 196 gt, 133 nt, 125.5 x 21.0 x 6.3 triple expansion steam engine 12, 19, 33 x 16. March, 1936 –J.F.S.

131 Motor fireboat *Alki*, steel, 1927, Oakland, Ca. 196 gt, 133 nt, 118.0 x 26.0 x 10.8.
Steamer *Vashona*, later *Sightseer*, and *Columbia Queen*, 1921 Tacoma, Wa. 185 gt, 145 nt, 110.1 x 22.9 x 6.5 triple-expansion steam engine 10, 16, 26 x 16 . 1937–J.F.S.

132–133 *Sightseer, as previously described.* December 5, 1937–J.F.S.

134 Steamer *Verona*, 1910 Dockton, Wa. 142 gt, 96 nt, 112.0 x 22.8 x 7.3. 1937–J.F.S.

135 Steamer *Atalanta*, 1913 Tacoma, Wa. 147 gt, 100 nt, 111.7 x 23.0 x 6.7. 1937–J.F.S.

136–137 Lake Washington Shipyard. 193–J.F.S.

138 Retired steamers at Lake Washington Shipyard. 1937–J.F.S.

139 Retired steamers at Lake Washington Shipyard. 1937–J.F.S.

140 Motor ferry *Chippewa*, steel, 1900 Toledo, Ohio 887 gt, 603 nt, 200.0 x 50.1 x 17.1. 1933–J.F.S.

141 Motor ferry *Chetzemoka*, ex-*Golden Poppy*, 1927, Almeda, Ca, 779 gt, 479 nt, 226.8 x 44.0 x 15.9.
   Steam ferry *San Mateo*, steel, 1922 San Francisco, Ca. 1782 gt, 1120 nt, 216.7 x 42.1 x 17.3 triple-expansion steam engine 19,32,54 x 36 1400 hp.,with 3 water tube boilers. September, 1969–J.S.S.

142 Ferry galley. 1935–J.F.S.

143 Motor ferry *Vashon*, 1930, Houghton, Wa. 641 gt, 436 nt, 191.3 x 56.9 x 15.1. 1933–J.F.S.

144 Motor ferry *Skansonia*, 1929, Gig Harbor, Wa. 446 gt, 303 nt, 158.4 x 49.9 x 13.3
   Motor ferry *Kalakala*, ex-*Peralta*, steel, 1927, Oakland, Ca. 1417 gt, 963 nt, 265.1 x 53.4 x 18.7. March, 1999 – J.S.S.

145 *Kalakala, as previously described.* July,1935–J.F.S.

146 Steam ferry *San Mateo, as previously described.* March, 1999–J.S.S.

147 *San Mateo, as previously described.* March, 1999–J.S.S.

148 *San Mateo, as previously described.* March, 1999–J.S.S.

149 *San Mateo, as previously described.* March, 1999–J.S.S.

150 Motor freighter *Belana*, 1928, Tacoma,Wa. 244 gt, 168 nt, 97.6 x 31.4 x 9.3 . 1933–J.F.S.

151 Motor freighter *Chimacum*, 1928, Olympia, Wa. 110 gt, 99 nt, 63.1 x 21.0 x 5.3
   Motor freighter *Capitol*, 1924, Dockton, Wa. 148 gt, 91 nt, 58.8 x 23.7 x 8.1
   Steamer *Mohawk*, 1921 Friday Harbor, Wa. 220 gt, 149 nt, 91.7 x 21.1 x 13.9. July, 1935–J.F.S.

152 *Capitol, as previously described.* 1938–J.F.S.

153 *Capitol, as previously described.* 1933–J.F.S.

154 Motor freighter *Warrior*, steel, 1936 Tacoma, Wa. 418 gt, 313 nt, 142.6 x 38.6 x 8.0. March, 1936–J.F.S.

155 *Warrior, as previously described.* March, 1936–J.F.S.

156 *Warrior, as previously described.* March, 1936–J.F.S.

157 *Warrior, as previously described.* March, 1936–J.F.S.

158 Motor freighter *Indian*, rebuilt from *L.P. Hosford*, steel, 1931, Portland, Or. 376 gt, 304 nt, 144.8 x 30.7 x 10.7 *Aleutian Native, as previously described.* May 23, 1938–J.F.S.

159 *Aleutian Native, as previously described.* May 23, 1938–J.F.S.

160 Motor freighter *Skookum Chief*, rebuilt from steamer *K.L.Ames*, 1915, Seattle, Wa. 251 gt, 185 nt, 119.5 x 30.1 x 7.0. January 16, 1935–J.F.S.

161 Motor freighter *F.E. Lovejoy*, steel, 1946, Olympia, Wa. 613 gt, 295 nt, 169.8 x 36.0 x 11.6. December, 1945–J.F.S.

162 *F.E. Lovejoy, as previously described.* December, 1945–J.F.S.

163 *F.E. Lovejoy, as previously described.* January, 1946–J.F.S.

164 Steam sternwheeler *Skagit Chief*, 1935, Seattle 502 gt, 469 nt, 165.0 x 40.1 x 6.4. September 3, 1938–J.F.S

165 *Skagit Chief, as previously described.* September 3, 1938–J.F.S.

166 Steam sternwheeler, *W.T.Preston*, steel, 1935, Seattle 291 tons displacement 161 ft-10 in x 33 ft-6 in x 5 ft-6 in. April, 1999–J.S.S.

167 Steam sternwheeler, *Portland*, steel, 1947 Portland, Or. 928 gt, 733 nt, 186.1 x 42.1 x 9.4. July,1999–J.S.S.

168 U.S. frigate *Constitition*, 1797, Boston, Ma. 2200 tons displacement 175.0 x 45.0 x 20.0. June 10, 1933–J.F.S.

169 *Constitution, as previously described.* June 10, 1933–J.F.S.

170 USS *SC-302*, 1917, Bremerton, Wa. 75 tons displacement 106.0 x 13.6 x 6.0. triple-screw Eastern Standard gas engines. April, 1918–J.F.S.

171 *SC 302*, deck view. 1918–J.S.S. setup.

172 USS APA-232 *San Saba*, steel, 1944 Vancouver, Wa. 7650 tons displacement 455.0 x 62.0 x 28.7. October, 1945–J.F.S.

173 USS Sargo class submarine *193*, Sworldfish, steel, 1939, Mare Is. 2,198 tons disp. sub. 310.6 OA x 26 x 16.8 draft January, 1940–J.F.S.

174 USCG cutter *Guard*, 1914, Mare Island, Ca. 52 tons

displacement 67.7 x 12.6 x 6.3. 1934–J.F.S.

175 USLHT *Heather*, steel, 1903, Seattle, Wa. 831 gt, 179.0 x 28.0 x 15.0. August 8, 1938–J.F.S.

176 USCG cutter *4323*, 1937. Stockton, Ca. 38 ft length. May 23, 1938–J.F.S.

177 USCG *AB-68*, 1936, Terminal Island, Ca. 56.0 x 14.8 x 4.0. May 23, 1938–J.F.S.

178 USLHT *Manzanita*, 1908 Camden, N.J. 1057 gt, 190.0 x 30.0 x 16.0. 1934–J.F.S.

179 USRC *Algonquin*, 1898 Cleveland, Ohio 736 tons displacement 1937–J.F.S.

180 Steamship *Canadian Princess*, ex-*William J. Stewart*, 1932, Collingwood, Ontario. 228 (overall) x 35 x 13.5 (draft). July, 1999–J.S.S.

181 USCG bark *Eagle*, ex *Horst Wessel*, steel, 1936, Hamburg, Germany. 1816 tons displacement, 265 ft (overall) x 39 x 17 (draft), 22 sails totaling 21,345 sq ft. August 3, 1965–J.S.S.

182 Motor vessel *Moby Dick*, ex-*Olympic*, *Preston H. Balliche*, 1914, Seattle, Wa. 38 gt, 32 nt, 61.7 x 13.8 x 6.4. September, 1939–J.F.S.

183 Motor vessel *Catalyst*, 1932, Seattle, Wa. 91 gt, (as built), 62 nt, 68.2 x 18.3 x 10.5. 1938–J.F.S.

184 Lightship *Swiftsure*, steel, 1930. 630 tons displacement 108.9 x 30.0 x 15.0. May 22, 1938–J.F.S.

185 Lightship *Swiftsure, as previously described.* 1972–J.S.S.

186 Fireboat *Duwamish*, steel, 1908, Richmond Beach, Wa. 309 gt, 210 nt, 113.0 x 28.1 x 14.1. January 1999–J.S.S.

187 Fireboat *Alki*, steel, 1927, Oakland, Ca. 196 gt, 133 nt, 118.0 x 26.0 x 10.8. June, 1999–J.S.S.

SNAPSHOTS

Clockwise from upper left, or top to bottom

188 1: Schooner *Wawona*, 1897, Fairhaven, Ca. 468 gt, 413 nt, 156.0 x 36.0 x 12.3. 1937–J.F.S.
2: *Wawona, as previously described.* July, 1999–J.S.S.
3: Auxiliary schooner *Robertson II, as previously described.* April, 1997–J.S.S.
4: Schooner *C.A. Thayer*, 1895, Fairhaven, Ca. 452 gt, 390 nt, 156.0 x 36.0 x 11.8

189 1: Dock at Hansville, Washington. 1934–J.F.S.
2: Steamer *Hyak*, 1909, Portland, Or. 207 gt, 141 nt, 132.2 x 20.8 x 5.5 triple-expansion steam engine 12, 18, 32 x 18, 750 hp. at 225 lbs. 1934–J.F.S.
3: Gas launch *Falcon*, 1908, Anacortes, Wa. 46 gt 26 nt,

67.9 x 14.9 x 4.8. 1920–J.F.S.

190 1: Gig Harbor, Washington. 1934–J.F.S.
2: Ferry *Vashonia*, ex-*Relief*, 1930, Gig Harbor, Wa. 211 gt, 179 nt, 93.2 x 38,0 x 11,8. 1938–J.F.S.
3: *Skansonia*, 1929, Gig Harbor, Wa. 446 gt, 303 nt, 158.4 x 49.9 x 13.3. January, 1999–J.S.S.

191 1: Kirkland, Washington ferry dock. October 15, 1913–J.F.S.
2: Motor ferry *Mt. Vernon*, 1916 Seattle, 168 gt, 114 nt, 101.5 x 31.0 x 10.5. 1934–J.F.S.
3: Eagledale, Washington. September, 1969–J.F.S
4: Motor ferry *Quillayute*, 1927, Winslow, Wa. 728 gt, 495 nt, 150.1 x 52.0 x 14.9

192 1: *Virgina V* engine. July, 1999–J.S.S
2: *Canadian Princess* engine. July, 1999–J.S.S.
3: *Portland* engine. July, 1999–J.S.S.
4: *San Mateo* boiler room. March, 1999–J.S.S.

193 1: Steamer *Skagit Belle* (wreck) 1941 Everett, Wa. 555 gt, 513 nt, 164.5 x 40.3 x 6.7. 1966–J.S.S.
2: Romano diving bell. 1933–J.F.S.
3: Steamships *Pacific Redwood* and *Pacific Spruce* hull plating. 1937–J.F.S.
4: *Foss 300*, steam powered crane. January, 1999–J.S.S.

194 1: Motor tug *Calumet*, 1934, Charleston, S.C. 186 gt, 127 nt, 104.5 x 24.0 x 11.4. May, 1979–J.S.S.
2: Motor tug, ex-YTM. 1979–J.S.S.
3: Motor tug *Elf*, ex *Foss 15*, ex-*Elf*, ex- *Skookum Cache*, 1902, Tacoma, Wa. 39 gt, 26 nt, 63.1 x 15.9 x 6.5 . June, 1999–J.S.S.
4: Motor tug *Gillking*, ex-*Columbia Queen*, 1942, Los Angeles, Ca. 99 gt, 81.1 x 21.3 x 9.7. 1979–J.S.S.

195 1: Motor tug *Marlin II*, ex-*Clayburn*, 1906. March, 1999–J.S.S.
2: Motor tug *Drew Foss*, 1929 Tacoma, Wa. 34 gt, 23 nt, 53.2 x 16.0 x 7.1. July 31, 1938–J.F.S.
3: Motor tug *Rustler*, 1887 Hoquiam, Wa. 20 gt, 13 nt, 53.0 x 13.9 x 4.6. March, 1999–J.S.S.
4: Motor tug *Arthur Foss, as previously described.*
Motor tug *F.L. Fulton*, 1955, Antioch, Ca. 71 gt 48 nt, 66.3 x 19.5 x 9.9.
Lightship *Swiftsure*, ex-*San Francisco*, ex-*Relief, No. LV 83*, later *No. WLV 508*, 1904, Camden, N.J. 668 gt (displacement), 188 nt, 112 ft-9 in x 28 ft-6 in x 14 ft-9 in compound engine 16, 31 x 24, producing 380 IHP at 120 rpm. January, 1999–J.S.S.

196 1: Motor tug *Favorite*, 1937, Tacoma 8 gt, 6 nt, 32.3 x 10.5 x 4.3. January, 1999–J.S.S.

2: Dunlap Towing chip barge and tug. March 29, 1999–J.S.S.

3: Merrill Ring Lumber Co. and steam tug *Tyee*, 1884, Port Ludlow, Wa. 316 gt, 158 nt, 141.2 x 26.4 x 13.0. 1935–J.F.S.

197 1: Motor tug *Sigrid H*, steel, ex-Army ST 74 x 20 x 9.1. March, 1999–J.S.S.

2: Tow winch of motor tug *Tyee*, *as previously described*. 1937–J.F.S.

3: Washington diesel. April, 1999–J.S.S.

4: Three ex-Army LTs, steel, 107.0 x 27.0 x 14.5. January, 1999–J.S.S.

198 1: Motor tug *Quail*, 1940, Koggiung, Alaska. 61 gt, 41 nt, 79.5 x 17.0 x 7.3. June, 1999–J.S.S.

2: Motor tug *North Bend*, 1973, Coos Bay, Or. 85 gt 58 nt, 66.4 x 21.5 x 9.8, steel. July, 1999–J.S.S.

3: Motor tug *Trio*, ex-*Trio*, ex-*Commando* 1911, Decatur, Wa. 37 gt, 23 nt, 55.2 x 15.3 x 6.6. June, 1999–J.S.S.

4: P.S.F.L. Terminal and tug *Anne Carlander*, 1972, Seattle. 140 gt, 455nt, 67.4 x 230.0 x 13.5. July, 1999–J.S.S.

199 1: Miki tug *Dominion*, ex- Army *LT366*, ex-*Patricia Foss*, 1944, Aberdeen, WA. 290 gt, 122 nt, 117.5 x 280.0 x 12.8. Single-screw Enterprise diesel 16 x 20, 1500 hp. April, 1997–J.S.S.

2: Motor tug *Koos No. 2*, 1924 Marshfield, Or. 13 gt, 9 nt, 49.7 x 12.8 x 3.7. July, 1999–J.S.S.

3: Launch *Hyack*, 1906, Dockton, Wa. 11 gt, 7 nt, 35.6 x 9.7 x 7.2. May, 1999–J.S.S.

4: Motor tug *Chickamauga*, 1915 Seattle 51 gt, 20 nt, 59.5 x 16.7 x 8.6. March, 1999–J.S.S.

200 1: Motor tug *Sandman*, 1910, Tacoma 28 gt, 19 nt, 49.0 x 14.0 x 6.5. May, 1999–J.S.S.

2: *Sandman* wheelhouse. May, 1999–J.S.S.

3: Motor tug *Palomar*, 1926, San Diego, Ca. 72 gt, 41 nt, 78.8 x 19.0 x 7.2. April, 1999–J.S.S.

4: Motor tug *Susan H*, 1947, Seattle 39 gt, 26 nt, 55.4 x 17.0 x 7.0. 198–J.S.S.

5: Motor tug *Joe*, ex-*Joe Foss*, 1942, Tacoma 15 gt, 19 nt, 43.0 x 14.4 x 4.9. May, 1999–J.S.S.

201 1: S.E.S.*Whidby*, ex-Army *T-482*, steel. December, 1997–J.S.S.

2: Passsenger launch *Plover*, 1944 Seattle 12 gt, 11 nt, 30.3 x 9.7 x 4.3. March, 1999–J.S.S.

3: M.V. *Pintail*, steel, 1948, Bellingham, Wa. 91 gt, 80 nt, 69.1 x 24.1 x 50.
M.V. *Nordland*, 1929, Hadlock, Wa. 34 gt, 30 nt, 58.1 x 22.4 x 3.2. February, 1999–J.S.S.

4: Gravel barge at Lopez Island, Wa. March 6, 1999–J.S.S.

202 1: H.M.C. S. *Cape Breton*, ex-H.M.C. S. *Flamborough Head*, steel, 1944, North Vancouver, B.C. Approx. 7100 gt, 441.6 x 57.2 x 27.8 (Canadian Victory Park type), triple-expansion steam engine 24.5, 37,70 x 48. July, 1999–J.S.S.

2: Motorship *Coho*, steel, 1959, Seattle, Wa. 5315 gt, 3846 nt, 310.3 x 68.0 x 15.9. June, 1999–J.S.S.

3: Steamship *W.M. Tupper*, steel 1917, Jacksonville, Fl. 1756 gt, 1092 nt, 217.6 x 38.0 x 23.6. 1934–J.F.S.

203 1: *Princess Marguerite's* stacks. September 9, 1989–J.S.S.

2: *Princess Marguerite's* pilothouse. September 9, 1989. J.S.S.

3: Steamship *Prince George*, steel, 1948, Esquimalt, B.C.; 5812 gt, 350.0 x 52.1 x 17.7 twin six-cylinder uniflow steam engines, 23 x 26. April, 1995–J.S.S.

204 1:View east from Ballard locks, Washington. 1937–J.F.S.

2: Motorship *Hie Maru*, steel, 1930 Japan 11,600 gt, 535 x 66 x 41. M.V. *Seatac*, 1926 Tacoma 302 gt, 221 nt, 107.4 x 32.7 x 9.3. January, 1940–J.F.S.

3: Steamship *President Madison*, steel, 1921 Camden, N.J. 14,187 gt, 8341 nt, 516.5 x 72.2 x 27.8. Luckenbach steamship, likely *Lena Luckenbach*. April 19,1933–J.F.S.

205 1: View southeast from Ballard locks, Seattle, Wa. October 5, 1935–J.F.S.

2: Steamships *Pacific Redwood*, and *Pacific Spruce*, *as above*. March, 1936–J.F.S.

3: Todd Pacific Shipyards. March 30, 1999–J.S.S.

206 1: Ships at Ballard, Washington. January, 1999–J.S.S.

2: *Catalyst*, *as previously described*. March, 1999–J.S.S.

3: *Arthur Foss*, *as previously described*. March,1999–J.S.S.

207 1: Reliable Steel Fabricators. March,1999–J.S.S.

2: R.S.F. crane. March,1999–J.S.S.

3: George Broom's Sons. January, 1999–J.S.S.

4: Lake Union Drydock. February, 1999–J.S.S.

208 1: Remains of *Sierra*. May 8, 1999–J.S.S.

2: Rosario, Orcas Island, Washington. Ca. 1916–J.F.S.

209 1: Steam Schooner *A.G.Lindsay*, 1889, Detroit, Mi. 1354 gt, 1111 nt, 198.4 x 37.6 x 21.8. C.1915-J.F.S.

2: Roche Harbor. C.1916-J.F.S.

210 1: Eagledale, near Winslow, Washington.
Motor ferry *Olympic* (retired) steel, 1938, Baltimore, Md. 773 gt, 308 nt, 198.2 x 60.1 x 13.0. February, 1999–J.S.S.

2: Snohomish River near Everett, Washington. Miki tug *Dominion*, *as previously described*.   April, 1999–J.S.S.

INDEX